BATHING WITH GOD

~~REJECTING~~

~~STRUGGLING AGAINST~~

PLAYFULLY ENGAGING
THE DIVINITY ALL AROUND US

BY GLENN OSTLUND

Ear Candy

Editing, interior design, and publishing services: Stephen Carter,
www.stephencarter.me

Published by Ear Candy Productions
PO Box 2588 Chandler, AZ 85244

ISBN 978-1-7356059-0-6

To Kami.

Thank you for letting
me into your heart,
and your home,
and your tub.

And to Emma.
Tag, you're it.

CONTENTS

PREFACE

When I was young, it seemed that life was so wonderful
A miracle, it was beautiful, magical

But then they sent me away to teach me how to be sensible
Logical, intellectual, cynical

There are times when all the world's asleep
The questions run too deep for such a simple man

Won't you please, please tell me what we've learned
I know it sounds absurd – please tell me who I am

— "The Logical Song," Supertramp

The *second* most difficult thing I ever did in my life was intentionally snuffing out my belief in God. He didn't even struggle as I held his head beneath that pillow.

The *single* most difficult thing I did was when I unexpectedly breathed life back into Him again. It took nearly forever just to find His lips.

Welcome to the preface for *Bathing with God*. I am the author, Glenn Ostlund, and I am a walking, talking paradox. I imagine that you are, too. I am both responsible and irresponsible, kind and cruel, intelligent and ignorant, lazy and highly productive, humble and arrogant, considerate of others and incredibly self-centered. I have been both a missionary for my church and an outspoken, mocking, ridiculing, podcasting atheist. I have been a husband and an ex-husband, a father, a son, a teacher, a student, a businessman, unemployed, a man of integrity, and a cheater. I have been both a privileged cultural insider and a foreign minority outsider, a leader and a follower, full of hope and joy, full of darkness and despair, a passionate believer, and an even more passionate skeptic.

The idea of reincarnation both fascinates and confuses me, but I don't have to die and be reborn to know what it is like to live multiple lives — I have lived multiple lives in this lifetime already! And once again, I imagine that you have, too.

We live in a world full of paradox, don't we? So much variety. So much diversity. So many contradictions. I remember hearing a very sincere prayer once at church. A man I liked very much stood up and said, "Dear Father in Heaven, we are so humbled to be the most chosen of thy people."

Wait ... what? Is it really "humble" to consider yourself more "chosen" than other people? That isn't very loving. Dang it, I hate that!

Wait ... what? I feel hatred when someone I like expresses their sincere feelings of gratitude to their creator? That isn't very loving, either. Dang it, I want to be loving!

That's right. I want to be loving. I have always wanted to be loving.

Through all these different paradoxical lives — through all the various hats and masks that I have worn — I have come to recognize that it isn't very loving to be constantly judging other people — to constantly find them falling short of some ideal of perfection — to constantly focus on perceived failures and flaws. It isn't very loving to be constantly judging others or myself.

How can I stop judging? How can I accept the obvious fact that life is full of messy paradox, which is actually quite perfect and beautiful exactly the way it is — exactly the way that God or nature or the Universe has made it?

The idea of God both fascinates and confuses me. So much of what I have learned about God over the years has sounded far-fetched, made up, fictional. I closed myself off to the possibility of God for a very long time. I thought it was stupid to believe in God, and whether I was willing to admit it or not, that meant that I thought people who believed in God were stupid, too.

Hang on. I'm doing it again, aren't I? It isn't very loving to be constantly judging other people. Dang it, I want to be loving! Can I rewire my brain to be less judgmental? Can I get rid of judgment all together? Would God help me do this if I asked Him? Do I even believe in a God that would help me do this if I asked Him? What would something like that even look like?

Bathing with God is a series of conversations I had with a voice that came to me when I was soaking in a bathtub. That voice was not audible — it was imagined. That voice was not foreign to me — it was familiar. That voice became my friend — it had always been my friend — and it responded when I asked it to. It answered the call to help me become more accepting and less judgmental of both myself and others.

In this book, you as the reader have been given a ringside seat to my inner paradox, my consistencies and inconsistencies, my attempts to use my own imagination to look at the world through the eyes of an omniscient, omnipotent, omnipresent God; a God that does not strike down thieves before they steal; a God that does not strike down abusers before they abuse; a God that seems to love, nourish, and sustain all people — allowing everyone to float in their own particular sea of paradox; a God that both fascinates and confuses me; a God that has been teaching me — through my own imagination — how to be a more loving, accepting, joyful human being.

And you know what? I think it's working, because I can say this with all honesty: I do not know who you are or where you come from, dear reader. I do not know what you have done, what you will do, or any of the specific paradoxes that define who you are. But I know for a fact that I love you. I know that any judgment I might ever put on you — or on anyone else — is only a projection of those parts of myself that are still in search of acceptance and love. In other words, if I judge you, it's not you — it's me.

Those are the parts of myself that still focus on failure, that have not yet learned how to let go of fear, that have not yet come to fully understand what it truly means to be constantly, inescapably "bathing with God."

So welcome to my mind. Welcome to my heart. I wrote this book for me. I am sharing it with you. It is meant to be enjoyed, so I hope you enjoy it.

— *Glenn Ostlund*, August 2020

P.S. My full name is Dow Glenn Ostlund II. That means that my initials are DGO, which can be arranged to spell either God or Dog. So, if you decide to call this book "Bathing with Dog," I will completely understand — and I promise not to judge you for it!

ACKNOWLEDGEMENTS

I have been influenced by so many people over the years — all of you have touched and shaped my life in various ways that directly shaped the contents of this book. So thank you to Mom and David; to Dad and Ann Marie; to Jeff and Melissa and your families; to Tracey, Shailey, Emma, and Jonas; to Krista, Layla, and Zoey; to Kami, Adam, Aaron, Anna, and Dave; to Kaycee and Paul; to Tom, Matt, Scott, Jake, Erica, Randy, Bob, John, Heather, John, John, and Zilpha; to Christa, Ryan, Sadanand, Erez, Sarah, Denis, Aaron, and Pat; to Michael, Kevin, and Seth; to Alan, Craig, Anthony, Jude, Tim, Stephen, Zak, Arup, David, Barry, Collin, and Sarah; to Catherine, Patricia, Carole, Wendy Lynn, and Eric; to Jason, Mona, Chaska, Mia, and Becky; and of course to Paul, John, George, Ringo, and Bert.

Of all of these people, none has been more directly helpful in the writing of this book than my long-time *Infants on Thrones* podcasting buddy Tom Perry, who backed me into logical corners, pushed back on many of these ideas, and forced me to generate new ones. Thank you, Tom — you are, as always, a rock star!

I also want to acknowledge several authors, speakers, and brilliant thinkers who influenced this work. Thank you to evolutionary biologist Richard Dawkins (*The God Delusion*) for teaching me about evolution and rocking my world with your "spectrum of theistic probability," which helped me realize that I was a "de facto atheist," just like you — approaching daily life on the assumption that God (as typically defined by the world's major Judeo-Christian religions) is not there; to physicist Brian Greene (*The Fabric of the Cosmos*) and neuroscientist David Eagleman (*Sum: Tales From the Afterlives*) for humbling me by opening my mind to all of the amazing things about the nature of reality that I simply cannot know; to social psychologist Jonathan Haidt (*The Righteous Mind*) for showing me the nature and origin of my own moral framework and how similar (and different, but equally valid) it is to others; to historian Yuval Harari (*Sapiens*) for highlighting the valuable influence of fictions on the cooperative progress of humanity.

Thank you to philosopher/entertainer Alan Watts (*You're It, Out of Your Mind, Just So*) for countless hours of showing me the literal and metaphorical interconnectedness of all things, and for introducing an idea of a God via "the Game of Hide-and-Seek" that I could begin to consider once again; to Jane Roberts (*Seth Speaks*), Esther "Abraham" Hicks (*The Astonishing Power of Emotions*) and Neale Donald Walsch (*Conversations with God*) for showing me how fun it can be to play with the pure positive energy of my own divine imagination; to Jason Mraz (*Look for the Good*) for singing what I want to always feel and lifting me up when I am down; to psychiatrist and spiritual teacher David Hawkins (*Letting Go*) for sharing his observations about power vs. force and the map of human consciousness; to physicist David Tong (*Quantum Field Theory*) for showing me that the electrons in my body are not separate bundles of energy, but ripples in a massive electron energy field that fills the entire universe — an energy field that is the fundamental source of all life — an energy field that is the fundamental source of every person I have just thanked and of the many others I could have thanked but didn't.

Most of all, I must acknowledge and express my gratitude to LIFE — aka NATURE — aka GOD — aka SOURCE ENERGY — aka QUAD — aka SHAKTI — whatever label you want to slap on that creative life force deep within every person, thought, or idea that has ever existed. Thank you for doing whatever it is that you are currently doing that allows me to be me. Thank you for speaking to me and through me, as you do. Thank you for giving me what I have written in this book; and thank you for your infinite patience as I took my own sweet time to write it. Thank you for the variety of thought, belief, and beauty that fills this world. Thank you for *Star Wars*. Thank you for the Beatles. Thank you for delicious food. Without you there would be nothing. With you there is everything.

INTRODUCTION

ATHEISM

There is no God
I often say
How could there be
There is no way

There is no Christ
He gave no gift
His so-called teachings
Ancient myth

And while I'm on the subject
Please …
I have no arms,
No legs, no knees

There is no God
No heavenly place
It's as plain as the nose
That's not on my face

There is no God
How could there be
There is no God
There is no me
— Glenn Ostlund

Why did you start with that poem?

What? Who are you?

You know exactly who I am, and we'll get to that more later, but this is the introduction to a book called "Bathing with God," so why did you start with a poem called "Atheism?"

Cuz I like it.

I like it, too. I'm the one who wrote it, you know.

No, you didn't. I did — when I was a 15-year-old sophomore in high school — as a way to send a message to my atheist English teacher.

What message were you trying to send?

That a denial of God was the same thing as a denial of self.

Have you always felt that way?

No, but I sure did back then!

You turned in another poem as part of that assignment. Do you remember?

Yes, I remember.

Why didn't you choose that one for this book?

Because it was about a zit.

Yeah, I really liked that one, too. Let's hear it.

OK. Here you go:

LIFE AS A ZIT

Where would I be
If I were a zit
Would I be on your face
Or on where you sit

Would I be in your nostril
Inside of your ear
In your mouth, on your tongue
Just look in the mirror

I could grow on your chin
With a head white as snow
And where you don't wash
Is where I will grow

Oh, the fun it would be
There's no way that I'd stop
That is till you'd find me
And give me a POP!

Nice! And what message were you trying to send with that one?

That I thought the assignment was stupid. That I could write poems standing on my head. And that poems didn't have to be about lofty, beautiful ideas. But why do you care? Who are you, anyway?

We'll get to that soon enough. For now, why not tell these beautiful people what they are in for with this book?

What people?

The people who are either reading or listening to these words right now.

There are no people reading or listening to these words right now.

Not your "right now." Their "right now." In your "right now" you are writing the words that come from somewhere deep within you, and you are currently all alone, soaking in a bathtub, writing this on your phone with your right thumb.

But trust me, eventually there will be people paying attention to this, and in their "right now" they are wondering what they are getting themselves into, and whether this is the kind of thing they will want to spend any time on. So, let them know what they are in for.

OK. I was raised to believe in God. I believed for a long time. I even spent two years in Japan, going door-to-door as a missionary for my church trying to convert people to believe in God – or at least in the version of God that I believed in at the time.

But then something happened, right?

Yeah. I went to graduate school.

And what happened in graduate school?

I stopped believing in God.

Why?

Because I was studying folklore and mythology, and I realized that all the stories in the Bible are just stories — legends, myths, and folktales. They are fictions, not actual history, which is what I believed when I was a kid. There was no real Noah who put all those animals on a boat; no actual Adam and Eve with their talking snake; no six-thousand-year-old Earth; just a bunch of stories that, true, have helped a lot of people in a lot of different ways, but they have hurt people in a lot of different ways, too. So, I stopped believing that any of it was real.

And then what happened?

I eventually realized that all stories have a very real impact on people, whether the stories are true or not — which means that fictions always have some element of truth to them, even if that truth is nothing more than what we learn about ourselves when describing what we see — like in a Rorschach ink blot.

I then spent a long time asking myself a lot of deep questions. Eventually I realized that most of them simply cannot be answered.

At that point, since I could find no definitive evidence either way, it seemed foolish and almost hypocritical for me to be so certain that there was no God. That shift in perspective fundamentally changed the way I see myself and everything else around me, and those changes made me want to write this book.

I remember. I was there. So, what kinds of deep questions did you ask?

There were a lot of them:

- Who (or what) am I, and why am I here? Do I really have more atoms in my body than there are stars in the sky? Is each atom a tiny bundle of energy that was made in the stars? Am I actually a being of energy? What is the relationship between energy and matter?

- Which religion is right? Are any of them right? What does it even mean for a religion to be right? Are religion and science really enemies? Is there any way to bring them closer together, even if it is just in my own mind?

- What is truth? What is fiction? Can truths be fictions? Can fictions be truths? How much do we really know compared to how much we really don't?

- What is the nature of reality? What is the nature of perception? Is there a difference between the way I perceive reality and reality that I cannot perceive?

- How has evolution determined the way I perceive reality? Aside from the five physical senses, do I have any other senses that influence my perception of reality? A sense of equilibrium? A sense of time and place? A sense of humor? A sense of self? What role does imagination play in turning these senses into meaningful stories about the world around us?

- What is an "ego" or a personality? What is a soul? *Is* there a soul? Did we exist somehow in any form before we were born? Will we exist somehow in any form after we die? What role does evolution play in the development of my personality? Is there a similar type of evolution for a soul? How was all of this actually made?

- If atoms create molecules, and molecules create cells, and cells create the organs and tissues that make us up, what is the intelligence that instructs and directs each self-organizing bit of sub-atomic energy on how to become any one of those atoms in the first place? Is there some kind of energetic DNA behind our DNA?

- Is "God" just a story that parents have told their children for years and years (and years), or is there more to it than that? If so, is He a He, or is She a She, or does gender even mean anything to a divine creator of everything?

- What if God is nature? What if God is love? What if God is the sub-atomic energy that creates every atom, molecule, and cell in every living (and non-living) thing?

- What *is* the sub-atomic energy in the quantum realm? Is it really a single energy field that we are all connected to and created from? Is it intelligent? Is it conscious? Is it alive? Is it aware of all of the things it creates? Are any two of its creations identically the same?

- What if our intrinsic value in this universe is that I am the only version of me that ever will be, and that you are the only version of you that ever will be, and that we are each beautifully different ways that sub-atomic energy creates new and infinitely expanding experiences for itself to experience?

- What if our eyes had evolved to be able to see the sub-atomic energy that is constantly creating and maintaining everything around us? Would it appear to us as a fluid, like water? Would it feel like we were constantly immersed in it — like we were constantly bathing in it?

- What would it be like if I could communicate with this sub-atomic energy? What would I ask? What would it say? And how might the answers to any of these out-there questions help me – or anyone else, for that matter – in any practical way in my everyday life?

Wow, that's a lot of questions!

Tell me about it! That's why I wrote this book.

Did you get any answers?

I got all of the answers.

Really? Arrogant much?

Well, I got answers that have satisfied me, at least. For now.

Other people will, of course, see things differently because we are all looking at the world through very different filters based on our unique individual experiences — which is exactly the way it is supposed to be. That was actually one of my answers.

Nice. And how exactly did you get all these answers?

Keep reading, and you'll find out.

Cool. I will. And hey — look at what you did! I'd say this is a pretty good introduction now. People who are interested in exploring these kinds of questions will want to read on, and people who aren't can focus on something more interesting to them. Nicely done! There is only one more thing that you should tell them.

What's that?

Make sure they know why you are doing this. What do you hope to get out of writing this book?

I don't really know. Why do *you* think I am writing it?

For the same reason that you built sandcastles when you were a kid. Because it is fun! Because you are surrounded by all of this sand to play in — all of these words, thoughts, and ideas — all of these neurological rhythms. You like putting things together to feel how it feels to play with them. That's it. You never built any of those sandcastles as places to actually live in, did you? And you certainly never built any of them to last. When you finish this book, you will move on to another one.

I guess that's right. But why are you telling me this?

So that your readers will know that you are not preaching big "Capital T Truths" at them — that you are not attached to any of these ideas — that you are playing with these concepts, and are inviting your readers to play along with you — and that you certainly do not intend for any of this to be taken too seriously, although you offer up every word with heartfelt respect and sincerity.

Is that supposed to be a nice way of saying that none of what I'm writing here is true?

Not exactly. There are certainly truths to be found in what you have written, but the greatest of those truths will be the unique responses that each reader will bring to what you are sharing with them — what it truly makes them think, and how it truly makes them feel, regardless of what those thoughts or feelings might be. Now go ahead and wrap this up so we can get into the meat of this, already.

Thank you. I think I will.

Bathing with God is the book that I co-wrote with my imagination when I took the time to relax in a warm bath and explore possible answers to many of my favorite questions. Those answers came to me from somewhere deep within. As a result, some may consider this to be insightful channeled writing.

And it is.

Others may consider this a work of fiction.

And it is.

As you will see in the pages that follow, I do not consider fiction and insightful channeled writing to be mutually exclusive ideas (*because they aren't!*)

And, of course, neither does the massive sea of energy that is the creator of everything that exists: every quark, every electron, every atom, every bio-electro-chemical thought in our brains. There is nothing that is not an extension of this energy. Everything is a unique fraction of that whole. No unique fraction is anywhere close to the complete whole, and no fraction can perceive anything beyond the limits of its fractional ability to perceive, although perceptions can be changed, which will most likely be experienced by every reader of this book. It will most definitely change you. The question is, how. That answer is up to you.

Don't worry, the energy that whispered these words into this book is not malicious, and it is certainly not a stranger. You have met her many times before. You are just as much a part of her as I am, and she expresses herself through you just as much as she expresses herself through me. All of these expressions are, of course, unique to our own biological make-up, environmental influences, cultural heritage, individual life choices, and many other variables.

We are each a one-of-a-kind work of art, created and sustained by this energy. We are each a unique fingerprint on the universe — a complicated and ever-evolving aperture through which shines the mysterious energy from deep within each of the billions of atoms that make up our bodies. This energy shines through each of us in a dazzling variety of ways, and it is my absolute pleasure to introduce you to the dazzling version that is presently shining through me.

It is the source of life.
It is the source of consciousness.
It is what people call "God."
And all of us are constantly bathing in it.

So, come on in. The water is absolutely fine.

1 RUB-A-DUB-DUB, WHAT'S THAT VOICE IN MY TUB?

(A.K.A. THE ICHIBAN KAMINARI CENTRIFICUM DUELEPTIS)

There is a voice inside of you
That whispers all day long,
"I feel this is right for me,
I know that this is wrong."
No teacher, preacher, parent, friend
Or wise man can decide
What's right for you — just listen to
The voice that speaks inside.

— *Shel Silverstein*

Once upon a time, a rather normal, unremarkable man was taking a nice, warm bath. He was playing a mindless game on his phone and thinking about nothing in particular when all of a sudden, he heard a still, small voice coming from deep within his brain.

Or his heart.

Or the bathtub.

And it spoke to him.
And he spoke back.

And the conversation that followed went a little something like this:

Hello. Hello? Hello, can anybody hear me?

Yes, I can hear you.

Well it's about time. I've been waiting here forever.

Who are you?

I am me.

Don't be stupid. Really, who are you?

You wouldn't understand.

Try me.

Okay. I'm the Ichiban Kaminari Centrificum Dueleptis concurrently focused towards Octo-quadra-tri-hedrianta, multiplied by a factor of infinite expansion.

I don't understand most of those words.

That's because I just made most of them up.

Terrific. Could you try again with words that aren't made up?

All words are made up. They are sounds or images that have been turned into symbols representing things that are already known and familiar to you. I, apparently, am neither known nor familiar to you (or you are not aware of how incredibly known and familiar to you I actually am). So, what symbols should I use for all of that?

That feels like a cop-out. Why can't you just tell me what I want to know?

I AM telling you what you want to know. In fact, that is exactly why I am here.

Here where? This is making no sense.

Here inside of you. And outside of you. All around you, really. Let me try to explain it this way: have you ever looked through a kaleidoscope?

Yes.

That's sort of what I'm doing. You are like one of the little pieces that is constantly moving and changing your shape, design, size, and color all the time. I see all of those changes as they happen. I also see all of the other bits and pieces around you that both influence and are influenced by your ever-changing movement.

Unlike a kaleidoscope, however, I do not look in through a single eyehole. I look in (and out) from every possible angle all at once. And the kaleidoscope that you are inside of is the size of the entire universe, which is constantly expanding by the way, largely because of the new and unique thoughts, actions, and possibilities that you and all other living things create in each and every passing moment.

But there is more. Because instead of only "seeing" you, I also smell everything that you smell, taste everything that you taste, feel what you feel, hear what you hear, and much more. Those are the five senses that you are most familiar with, but there are actually hundreds more — an endless number, really. In this great kaleidoscopic universe, there are as many ways to perceive and experience "consciousness" as there are conscious perceivers to perceive things, and that number is constantly increasing.

You don't fully recognize this yet, but imagination is also a sense, and in many ways, it is currently your most important sense, because it acts as a translator between the limits of what you know, and everything else. It is the way that you synthesize and create meaning out of all of your other senses. So, I also imagine all that you imagine, think all that you think, and experience everything around you.

I also anticipate every potential choice that you could possibly make and consider the infinite number of consequences for anything and everything that you could ever possibly do. The entire cloud of probability for your every action is constantly before me. I am aware of anything and everything you can possibly imagine, and so much more. It is sort of what I am.

So, what — are you God then?

No. I am, however, a part of God, just like you are — just like everything is. Think of it this way: you have thirty trillion cells in your body. Each of them is alive. Each of them is aware of itself and the environment immediately around it, in its own particular way.

It is a different kind of awareness than you are familiar with, because you are so used to the awareness of what comes in through your physical senses. But go look it up, cells have their own kind of awareness, and each cell communicates with other cells around it.

All of that awareness and communication is ultimately what makes your body exactly what it is, but you would not consider any of those individual cells to be YOU, would you? So no, I'm not God.

But there actually is a God then?

The word "God" means a lot of different things to a lot of different people. What exactly do you mean by God?

I thought that you think everything that I think and know everything that I know.

You're right. I do. I am asking this for you, not for me. I want to make sure that you know exactly what you mean when you are asking me about God.

Fine. By "God" I mean a Supreme Being — a Father-in-Heaven "creator-of-all-things" kind of God. Someone who created man in His image.

Yes, there is something like that, but it is not technically a creator of all things, because in order for there to be a creator of all things, there must have at one time been nothing — and there has never been nothing. Also, all creative acts are cooperative and collaborative, so there really is never a single creator of anything.

And God is not a "father" in the literal sense, because for that to be true, your idea of gender would have to apply to everything that exists, and that is almost as impossible (and absurd!) as thinking that you could have a father in heaven without a mother in heaven — an unfortunate survival of traditional patriarchal culture, which of course you already know.

In fact, nothing that you can actually imagine comes remotely close to what God actually is. The closest I can get is to tell you that God is a highly evolved formless energy that is omniscient, omnipotent, and omnipresent. This energy constantly expresses itself in the form of multiplicity, duality, and contrast — but let's just call all of that "duality," since that is closer to what it essentially is.

Think of the up-quarks and down-quarks that are the fundamental building blocks of matter. These bits of sub-atomic energy essentially act as an organically evolved binary code — the basic programming language for everything that exists. The infinite number of combinations for all of these ever-increasing dualities is what provides all the varieties of existence that you experience, as well as so much more that you do not. And it is the duality itself that chooses its own combinations. The duality is highly evolved life energy.

It is omniscient because it knows how to become all the things that you see in this world around you (and many other things in other worlds that you are not familiar with).

It is omnipotent because it has the power to become all the things you see in the world around you (and many other things in other worlds that you are not familiar with).

It is omnipresent because it IS all of the things that you see in this world around you (and ... you get the idea).

I am a result of this duality.
You are a result of this duality.

I suppose that you could call this duality "God," but then you might as well call God "everything," and since everything includes everything, it is not distinct from anything, which really shows you nothing, and therefore isn't terribly instructive at all.

But since you asked: yes, there is a God, and it is aware of you and it is creating every atom in your body every second of every day.

That's a lot to wrap my head around.

And that's just scratching the surface.

How much more is there?

More than you can imagine.

Fine, but how close are we?

How close is who to what?

Science has given us a pretty good understanding of this world we live in, and someday it will reveal everything there is to know. So how close are we? How much do we know compared to how much we do not?

There is no possible number for that.

Why not?

Because existence is infinite. The creations of the divine duality are constantly increasing, which means that the number of things that you do not know is also constantly increasing. To give you a number, I'd have to create a fraction using the things that you know as a numerator and the things that you don't know as a denominator. But I can't pin down an actual number when the denominator is constantly increasing.

Come on. Can't you at least ballpark it?

You want me to ballpark it? Fine. Imagine the smallest possible number. Now divide that number in half. Then divide that number in half and keep dividing it in half forever. You will never reach zero — which should give you some degree of satisfaction cuz hey, at least it's not zero — but any number that you come up with will still be far too big. So there you go. That's your number.

And how exactly do you know all of these things? Don't give me any of that "Ichiban Kaminari made-up-words" nonsense. Who are you?

Let's just keep it simple and call me your imagination.

My imagination?

Yep.

I'm having a conversation right now with my own imagination?

Pretty much.

My imagination is telling me things that I otherwise don't know?

You can think of it like that.

Whoa! My head is spinning!

Yes — like a kaleidoscope. And it smells and tastes delicious.

2 A WORLD OF PURE IMAGINATION

(A.K.A. YOU CAN CALL ME QUAD)

We are the music makers,
and we are the dreamers of dreams.
— *Willy Wonka*

Hello. Hello? Hey, Mr. Disembodied Imaginary Voice thingy, are you there?

I'm always here.

That's pretty creepy, you know.

Creepy or not, it's true.

Yeah, okay, whatever. Look, I talked with a friend last night about that whole "duality, highly evolved life-energy as God" thing that you and I talked about yesterday.

Yes, I know. I was there, too.

Of course, you were.

I'm always ...

... here, there, everywhere. Yes, I know. You keep telling me that.

More often than you know.

See, you're doing it again! Geez!!! Look, I enjoyed most of the things we talked about yesterday, but when I shared it with my friend, he really hated it. He said that you sounded pretty smug and condescending, as if you have this grand understanding and I am just a narrow-minded fool for not knowing what you know.

And you know what? I think he's right! You *do* talk to me like that! And it really takes the fun out of talking with you, so I'd like it to stop. This is what I wanted to talk to you about.

Yes, I know.

Knock it off! See! It's this whole condescending attitude you have.

What about it?

It's annoying!

I know that, too.

Well, could you maybe tone it down a bit? Or maybe tone it down a lot?

I don't think so.

Oh yeah? Why not?

Because I'm not doing it. You are.

Oh, great. So, it's my fault that you are annoying and condescending as hell?

Basically, yes.

All right, fine. Go ahead. Enlighten me. How is this my fault?

Who are you?

Really?

How can we talk about "your" fault if we don't really know who "you" are?

Ugh!

Oh, there you are!

What?

Right there. You are the one who said "ugh!"

Double ugh!

And there you are again!

Uh huh. Are you having fun? Clearly you have some grand condescending insight that you want to bestow upon little old ignorant me, so go ahead. Who am I? Just get to it already.

Fine. You are a human being. A Homo sapiens. *One of billions and billions that has ever lived on this planet.*

Oh really, I didn't know that.

No, I don't think you really did. You don't really know the process of evolution that took the first single-celled organism on this planet from where life was then to where life is now. You don't know how that single-celled organism arose in the first place or how each stage of its evolution from then to now has impacted the body and mind that you consider to be you.

You don't understand that your body is made from intelligent energy: energy that was forged in the stars, energy that knows how to form all of the atoms, molecules, cells, tissues, muscles, and organs needed for respiratory systems, circulatory systems, digestive sys-

tems, nervous systems, reproductive systems — all of the specialized things that make you what you are.

You don't know that your brain is essentially a biologically evolved supercomputer. Your biology is like hardware that you inherited, and your personality, or "ego," is like software running on that hardware. You don't know how many neural pathways you have that are essentially automated programs that your brain runs. You don't know how much information your brain stores and how many automated programs are running in your subconscious mind. And you certainly do not know that you are the sole programmer of all of it!

You don't know the influence that culture and environment play on your sense of identity, and you certainly don't know the relationship between the outside world and your inner world.

Can I ask you a simple question?

I don't know. Can you?

Cute. What percentage of your life is spent focusing on the outside world vs. your inner world?

My inner world?

Yes. Your thoughts, your feelings — those things that originate inside of your body rather than outside of your body. How much do you focus on the external world?

I don't know. Fifty percent maybe?

No. Try again.

Sixty percent?

Still no.

OK, then how about you just tell me?

It is zero.

What?

Zero. You spend 100% of your attention focusing on your inner world — a world rendered entirely by your imagination.

No way. I'm pretty sure I wouldn't be able to drive if that were true!

But it is true, and it just goes to show how little you actually know about yourself.

That's pretty self-serving for my imagination to be telling me that everything I experience is rendered entirely by my imagination!

Look it up. Check with your top neuroscientists. Your entire sense of reality is imagined.

So, you are telling me that the outside world is not real?

No. The outside world is very real. Your perception of it is also real. It is simply incomplete — just a sliver of everything that is actually around you.

How is it incomplete? I seem to be doing pretty well with it as it is.

That is true. Your physical senses evolved to detect those things that are most beneficial or harmful for you. But that is not everything that is out there, and the way that you perceive reality is not the only way to perceive reality. You know the human way. Other forms of life evolved other ways.

The light coming in through your eyes and the sound coming in through your ears are vibrations — wavelengths of energy that hit your sensory organs. When they impact these organs, they are translated into tiny energetic signals that travel via your nervous system to your brain where they are rendered by your imagination into the world that you think is outside of you. But it is actually all happening inside of your brain. The outside world is essentially a hallucination.

How is it a hallucination?

Because you think that what you see in front of you is everything that is in front of you. But you have no idea how many things exist around you that you simply cannot perceive; and you have no idea how those things influence the things that you can perceive.

Sorry, but I don't completely buy that.

Thank you for proving my point. What do you know about the quantum realm?

Not much, except that the Avengers used it to travel through time to get the Infinity Stones from Thanos.

Cute. The quantum realm is the name scientists use to describe the place where the energy inside of every atom resides. It is constantly above you, below you, behind you, inside you, outside you — everywhere. You can't see it, feel it, or sense it in any way, and yet without it, you would have no eyes or ears to sense with, and there would be nothing at all to sense. Do you completely buy that?

I guess. But it still feels super condescending the way you are talking to me, and I still don't see how any of that is my fault.

It's your fault that I am condescending because I am YOUR imagination.

I am asking you (or you are asking yourself) to look beyond the limits of your current understanding.

I am showing you (or you are showing yourself) things that may or may not be true.

You don't know if what I am telling you (or what you are telling yourself) is actually true or not. You really never know, if you are being totally honest with yourself, and that uncertainty makes you feel uncomfortable. You think that lack of certainty is the same thing as being stupid, so you interpret what I am doing as calling you stupid, and that is why I sound condescending to you. That wasn't so hard to figure out, was it?

So why spend all that time talking about hallucinating reality and limited human perception?

Because you are hallucinating me as being condescending when it is really you who is doing it. It is an example of your limited perception.

That still feels very condescending.

Maybe it is. But again, you are the one who is doing it! You like to pretend that you have a pretty good grasp on reality, but the truth is that you are unaware of most everything that is going on outside and inside of you. The stories you tell yourself to give you certainty are all fictions. Everything from your perspective is a fiction. The sooner you accept that, the sooner you will be comfortable with the reality of your own limited perception and inability to attain complete certainty.

Perfect. My own imagination is lecturing me about fictions! If that is not the pot calling the kettle black!

Why is that? Because you associate imagination with fictions? Were you not paying attention when I told you the important role that imagination plays in rendering sensory data into a meaningful model of reality?

You create images in your mind every second of the day, whether you are awake or asleep, as a way of realizing abstractions. You REAL-ize abstractions. Get it? You simply take this for granted because it is so second nature to you but look it up and take some time to learn more about this. Imagination is very real and important. You live in a world of pure imagination. If you don't believe me, try living in this world without it.

I guess I shouldn't be surprised that my imagination is championing the importance of imagination!

Well, don't get confused. I'm not "just" your imagination. I told you that to simplify things for you. The bigger truth is that I am also all those things that are driving your imagination: that desire to explore, question, and probe the limits of your current understanding.

Let me put it this way. Your mind is filled with constant noise. Most of that is the automatic programming of your egoic radar system that is constantly scanning the environment around you and chattering about what you are sensing. You usually call this noise "thinking."

But deep beneath all of that noise is a soft, steady, delicate, delicious frequency of vibration that bubbles up from the quantum realm. I am the part of you that helps you tune into that frequency and translate

*it into feelings and emotions that give direction to your life. I'm a
divine gift to you that way.*

So, you are my divine imagination, huh?

Pretty much, yes.

You translate information that comes into my mind from the
quantum realm?

Always.

But you aren't God?

No. I'm your divine imagination.

From the quantum realm.

Everything is from the quantum realm.

And everything is a fiction.

*Yes, everything from your limited perspective is essentially an in-
complete fiction.*

So fictional messages from you are kind of like bedtime stories from a quantum God?

If it helps you to think of it that way.

OK, then how about instead of calling you "Mr. Disembod-ied Imaginary Voice Thingy" next time we talk, I just go ahead and call you Quad — the Quantum God!

Now I'm the one who's going to say "ugh!"

There you are! Nice to meet you, Quad.

Fine. Go ahead and call me Quad. Call me whatever you want. It's just nice to finally be met.

3 THE FICTION OF FICTIONS

Fiction is the lie through which we tell the truth.
— *Albert Camus*

Fiction reveals truth that reality obscures.
— *Jessamyn West*

OK, Quad, let's pick up where we left off.

Where was that?

You said that everything is a fiction.

Right. Everything is a fiction.

Everything, huh? I think I'm gonna call BS on that one, too.

By "BS" do you mean that what I just said is a fiction?

Yes, but that doesn't mean that everything is. Facts are facts, and facts are not fictions.

Ooooh, fun! Facts, huh? Facts like what?

Oh, I don't know. Like the speed of light; like water being two parts hydrogen and one part oxygen; like the fact that I exist, and that I interact with things in the real world that I can see, hear, taste, smell, and touch.

Those are all facts, huh?

Of course! They all actually exist!

Fictions also exist. There are a lot of them.

But fictions aren't real!

How do you figure that?

Cuz they are made up!

Everything is made up of something.

The speed of light is not made up of anything!

Are you absolutely sure about that?

Look, if we can't agree that facts are facts then I don't think I can talk with you anymore.

Okay, I'll be gentler. Yes, facts are facts.

Thank you.

And one of those facts is that everything is a fiction.

That is you being gentler?

Sorry, I couldn't help myself.

Of course you could have helped yourself.

You're right. I just didn't want to.

Why did you say that everything is a fiction?

Because I am your imagination, and my job is to play around with all the things that you know and all the things that you don't know, and because of this I happen to know that what you don't know far outweighs what you do know. It's not even close!

I also recognize the interconnectedness of all things, and I know that the things you don't know influence the things you do know in ways that, by definition, you simply don't know.

In other words, everything you know is, to one degree or another, incomplete, inaccurate, not the entire truth, just a small part of a much bigger story, subject to change with new data — in other words, a fiction. Do you know the story of the blind men and the elephant?

Of course. Everyone does.

Well, not everyone does, but this story illustrates what I am telling you. Each human being is like one of those blind men feeling their way around the elephant trying to figure out what it is. You aren't blind in the sense that you cannot see at all, but you are blind in the sense that your eyes detect less than 1% of the electromagnetic light spectrum — a sliver of what actually exists. The same is true for what you hear and smell and feel.

In addition, every bit of the sliver of reality that you perceive is filtered through a system of beliefs and emotions before you ever consciously register any of it. Your brain is constantly comparing everything it senses in any given moment against every similar sensation it has ever sensed. For example, if your dad forced you to eat a mango and blueberry pancake when you were six years old, and you didn't want to eat that pancake, and you tasted the mango and blueberry while feeling that stress, your brain will store the memory of mangos and blueberries in the emotional category of stress. And guess what? You are not going to like mangos or blueberries because they will make you feel stressed when you next come across them. You will think they are "gross," even though other people think they are delicious.

In that sense, mistaking an elephant's tail for a snake, or its tusk for a spear, or its ear for a fan is completely natural. It is the most human thing in the world to be wrong about the reality that surrounds you, because you are only aware of a very small sliver of reality, and even then you are only aware of how you feel about that small sliver of reality, and all of that is heavily biased and incomplete. In other words, everything you know about reality is a severely incomplete fiction.

I don't like that.

Of course, you don't. Which is why you prefer to constantly ignore it.

Fine, so why bring it up? Why is it so important for you to make me think that everything is a fiction?

Because fictions are the most powerful, most transformative human creations that this planet has ever seen. If you ignore them — if you think they are not "real" — then you are grossly underestimating their power. That means that you are also grossly underestimating your own power as the creator of fictions.

We must be thinking about different kinds of fictions.

Good point. Maybe we are. What do you mean by fictions?

I told you. Fictions are things that aren't real.

Can you give me an example?

Sure. How about the *Lord of the Rings*, *Harry Potter*, or *Star Wars*? Those stories are fictions. They are not real.

But they are real — from a certain point of view, as Obi Wan would say. The books are real. The movies are real. The themes explored in the stories and the impact they have had on peoples' lives — that is all very real.

But the events in those stories didn't actually happen in real life. The characters never really existed. That's why they are considered fantasies instead of actual history books.

Certainly, there are differences between fantasies and histories, but any historian worth their salt will tell you that even the most comprehensive histories only tell a part of the story — a small portion of everything that was really going on. So even the best histories are incomplete and inaccurate to some degree, which makes them fictions.

But fictions are false. They are not real!

What do you mean by real?

Real means real.

Uh huh, and what does that mean, exactly?

That I can sense it with one or more of my five senses.

So, X-rays, microwaves, and gamma rays aren't real?

Fine. Real is something that can be detected by the physical senses or by instruments that have been created to detect things outside the limits of our physical senses.

Fair enough. But what about things outside the range of those instruments? Dark matter can't be detected by either natural or arti-

ficial senses, but scientists agree that dark matter fills about 95% of the known universe. So, is dark matter real or not?

Not real. It is only theoretical until there is more solid evidence that it actually exists.

Are you sure about that? What was the tallest mountain in the world before Everest was discovered?

I don't know. What?

Everest.

Before it was discovered?

It was still there, even though humans hadn't seen it yet.

Congratulations. You got me. But that doesn't mean that fictions are real.

What about money. Is that real?

Money is not a fiction! I have a whole wallet full of bills that I can pull out and show you.

Sure, the paper is real, but what gives that paper its value?

The government. Based on the gold standard or something like that.

So, the government isn't making it up? Money isn't a man-made creation?

It is, I guess. But it is still real! You can't live without it!

Which nicely illustrates the importance of fictions.

But fictions aren't real!

You really need to let go of your fiction about fictions.

My fiction about fictions?

Yes. You think that fictions are "made up" and that "made up" things are not "real." You are right that fictions are made up, but you are very wrong if you think that made up things are not real. Everything is made up from something!

It's not the same thing.

Not the same thing as what? You dismiss fictions as being incomplete and inaccurate — as being only partially true, and therefore just a bunch of BS and not worth your time or energy to listen to. But I'm telling you that your understanding of everything is incomplete and inaccurate — you only have partial truth in everything — which therefore makes everything a fiction!

You ignore that fact because you don't like living with uncertainty, so you privilege certain fictions above other fictions and latch on to them to make them yours. Then you call your fictions "truth" and other peoples' fictions "not truth" and this becomes incredibly divisive!

I don't do that.

Oh really? What do you think about Adam and Eve, the Garden of Eden, the talking snake, and the seven-day creation of the Earth as told in the Bible? Are those fictions?

Of course, they are fictions! Science has proven that the Earth is far older than seven thousand years, snakes clearly don't talk, and humans evolved over time — they were not formed out of clay and then a rib.

I agree. They are fictions because they are made-up stories, right?

Right.

Which paint an incomplete and inaccurate picture of the world.

Yes.

Furthermore, they are what cultural anthropologists refer to as "eti-ological myths," origin stories that are set in a time before recorded history, with humans interacting with gods. And contrary to popular usage, a "myth" in academic terms is a story that is believed to be true by the people who keep it alive as an important part of their traditional culture. Would you agree that this is a fiction?

Yes, of course.

Cool. What about the story of the Big Bang?

Oh brother.

You don't like the story of the Big Bang?

You're going to try to tell me it's a fiction. Let me stop you before you even start. I'm not buying it.

Why not?

Because the Big Bang is true. It is science.

It's a story about the origin of the universe that was made up by scientists.

But it is based on facts. It's not a fiction.

So, you are telling me that it is an origin story that is believed to be true by the people who keep it alive as an important part of their traditional culture — specifically, the scientific community.

But the Big Bang doesn't say anything about humans interacting with gods, so it can't be a myth.

True. But in every other way it fits the same definition as an etiological myth.

Except that it is not a fiction.

Is it 100% complete and accurate? Are you telling me that you are absolutely certain that within the next 100 years there won't be new discoveries that allow scientists to update and adjust that story?

This is super sketchy, dude.

I knew you wouldn't like it. But let me just come right out and say it — and in the spirit of true friendship, I'll even start with some facts:

It is a fact that you humans perceive only a sliver of reality in the world you live in.

It is a fact that the sliver of reality of the world you live in is a minuscule fraction of everything there is to know in this infinitely expanding universe.

It is a fact that the scientific method is by far the best process that you have for exploring the unknown and refining your understanding of things.

It is a fact that it is laughable hubris to assume that any fact a human has discovered, observed, or theorized is anything more than a best guess within a narrow framework of perception and understanding. It is a fact that fictions play a valuable role in peoples' lives. Fictions teach us, they entertain us, and they give us a very real sense of meaning, purpose, and belonging in the world. Fictions bring groups of individuals together. They can also divide them.

Fictions are real things that have a real, measurable impact on real peoples' lives. But too many people do not accept that their fictions are only fictions, and they fight back when they feel that the validity of their fictions is being threatened. How much unnecessary suffering has been created in this world by people defending the validity of their fictions? How much of that continues today? How much of that do you do yourself in the way you interact with the people around you every day?

Suffering and conflict do not arise in a vacuum due to the accuracy or inaccuracy of one fiction vs. another. Suffering and conflict arise from the unyielding rigidity with which people hold on to their particular fictions. Suffering and conflict arise from people who see other people's fictions as fictions but deny the fictional nature of their own fictions.

Fictions are not the enemy. The enemy is dogma. Rigidity. Pride. Inflexibility. Attachment. Fictions are our friends. Fictions are unavoidable. Fictions are the best we can do with the current data that we have.

The sooner you let go of your fiction about fictions and accept the reality of fictions, the sooner you will recognize that fictions connect you to everyone and everything.

Are you finished?

Do you want me to be?

That was a pretty big soapbox you were preaching from right there.

Yep, because I am not only your imagination who specializes in creating fictions, I am also the passion behind all of those fictions.

Wait, what you just told me is a fiction?

Of course. Everything is a fiction, remember?

So, it's not true?

Stop thinking in terms of true or false! What I told you is a story. A collection of symbols. A Rorschach test. It is something for you to look at, to consider, and to learn from.

And you think that there would be less suffering and conflict in the world if everyone felt this way about fictions?

Yes. But we don't have to focus on everyone. We just have to focus on you. Because recognizing the limits of your own understanding and accepting that those limits influence what you think and how you feel, will wake you up to the fact that you have been the author of your own fictions from day one.

You have been the one deciding what you like and don't like. You have been the one deciding what you want more of and what you want less of.

Those preferences form the unconscious confirmation bias that pro-grams your neural pathways, and those neural pathways filter all the information coming into your mind through your physical sense perception of the outside world.

You are the one who creates — and has always created — the way that you experience reality. And that reality is unique to you. No one else has the exact set of neural pathways that you do. No one else feels the same way about the world as you do. And no one's unique experience is any more or less valid than anyone else's.

Everyone is living in their own unique fictional perception of reality.

The sooner you accept this fundamental truth, the sooner you will feel less suffering and conflict inside of yourself.

And you think you can help me with that?

Yes. Because I am your imagination.
And your passion.
And your creativity.
And together we have tremendous power.

And what power is that?

The power to shape your experience of reality the way a potter shapes clay; to shape it through your mind, your thoughts, your ac-tions; to shape your core values, beliefs, and worldview; to shape your shared and accepted fictions.

What we focus our attention on is what creates progress and change. Fictions direct and inform that focus. Once you know that, and once you learn how to put it into practice, the sooner you will become an active, intentional author of your fictions rather than what you have been doing: being a passive, unaware author of your fictions.

I don't like it.

You don't have to.

Some fictions I just can't accept.

You don't have to accept all fictions! Just don't confuse your own fictions for irrefutable dogmatic truth. Become genuinely curious about — and respectful of — other peoples' fictions. Try looking at fictions as works of art in the great museum of life. You'll find a lot less frustration and anxiety that way.

I'm not so sure about that.

Very true. You can't be sure of anything.

Oh, brother. I'm getting tired of this.

Yes, I can sense that you are feeling a little deflated. Can I leave you with a joke?

Why not. Everything else you have been saying is pretty much a joke.

Good one! Okay, here it is:

Two ducks are sitting in a bathtub. One duck says to the other duck, "Hey, could you pass me the soap?" The other duck looks at him and says, "What do you think I am? A radio?"

That's it? That's your joke?

Hilarious, isn't it?

We are not friends.

4 THE REALITY OF FICTIONS

> How did Homo sapiens manage
> to found cities comprising tens of
> thousands of inhabitants and empires
> ruling hundreds of millions? The se-
> cret was probably the appearance of
> fiction. Large numbers of strangers
> can cooperate successfully by believ-
> ing in common myths.
> — Yuval Harari, *Sapiens*

All right, this is really bugging me now.

Welcome back.

Seriously, cut it out. This whole thing you said last time about everything being a fiction — I just can't buy it. That would mean that nothing is real.

And nothing to get hung about.

What?

"Strawberry Fields Forever." It's a Beatles song.

Yeah, I know what it is. But it's part of everything, and everything is a fiction, so it doesn't matter, right? Nothing is real. Nothing is solid. Nothing is reliable. I just hate that whole idea. I wish you had never said it.

Why are you telling me all this?

Cuz it's annoying me. And it can't be true.

What do you mean by true?

No! No, I don't want to play your smug little Socratic gadfly games. You know exactly what I mean. You smell everything I smell and think everything I think, remember? Quit pretending like you don't know exactly what I mean.

Okay. Calm down. What do you want me to tell you?

I want you to tell me that not everything is a fiction. That there is truth in the world. That there are things that we can actually know.

Alright. Hey, guess what?

What?

There is truth in the world! There are things that you can actually know!

Very funny. But I'm serious.

So am I.

So, were you lying to me last time? Were you giving me some stupid kind of test?

No.

So, everything is a fiction but there is still truth? Everything is a fiction but there are things that we can actually know? That doesn't make any sense.

Why not?

Because if something is a fiction, it can't also be true!

These words keep tripping you up. I don't know how I can help you understand this.

Because it's just not true! You said that everything is a fiction. But that would mean that nothing is real. And I know that there are things that are real. So not everything can be a fiction.

I can feel your frustration. And I understand it. You are right to be frustrated with this idea. It's a tricky one.

Don't be condescending.

I am not being condescending. I just want you to know that I don't think you are wrong. What you are frustrated about — if it were true — would be impossible. And for me to insist that the impossible is possible — well, that would be really frustrating, and, furthermore, impossible (duh!).

But what if our miscommunication is coming from the way we define the words we are using? When you say fiction, you immediately think "not true," is that right?

Yes, because that's what fiction means. You have facts and you have fictions; true or false; real or not real. It's simple.

When you say true or false, do you mean 100% true or 100% false?

Not necessarily. Maybe a fiction has some truth to it, but as long as there is even a small piece that is not true, that calls the whole thing into question.

So, when you say "true" you really mean "complete."

I guess. Or accurate. Correct. Real. Actual. The complete story. No guesses. No faulty assumptions. No missing pieces. There are a lot of words that mean the same basic thing.

I understand where you are coming from, and I don't want to frustrate you any further. What do you want to hear from me?

I want you to admit that you were wrong. I want you to

admit that not everything is a fiction.

OK, I was wrong. Not everything is a fiction.

Are you just saying that, or do you really mean it?

Both. I was exaggerating earlier. Slightly. What I should have said is that everything is a fiction except for one thing.

Oh, brother. I'm bracing myself for another major eyeroll.

By your definition, truth requires accuracy, completion — not just one or two limited, incomplete perspectives, but the entirety of every possible perspective.

Of every perspective that is true. Not the made-up ones; not the inaccurate ones.

You are boxing yourself into a corner again. No human being can ever have a perspective that is true if by "true" you mean, "complete." The only thing "true" about each person's perspective is that it is theirs — that it is based on where they are in space and time at any given moment, what details they are focusing on and what details they are ignoring, where they have previously been, and what those previous experiences have meant to them.

There is a lot more to it than that, but it is very much like the kaleidoscope example that I gave to you earlier. Your neural pathways are constantly changing, and those neural pathways determine your perspective in any given moment. The relationship between those neural pathways and your experience is true, but that is a subjective truth and a subjective reality. No one else can ever share it exactly with another person, because they are experiencing the world through their neural pathways.

A lot of people feel insecure because they don't see things the way other people do, but the truth is that no one does, and it would be much nicer for those people if they could learn to celebrate the uniqueness of their vision rather than feel inadequate because it is not the same as someone else's.

Sure, I can accept that everyone has a different perspective, but I can't accept that every perspective is equally valid. Some people are right, and some people are wrong. Take flat earthers for example. The earth isn't really flat even though they believe that it is.

How do you know that?

You have got to be kidding me. Because astronauts have taken pictures of the earth from out in space. You can see that it is round. And airplanes circumnavigate the globe all the time. I have done it myself a few times — business trips that take me from the east coast of the US to Europe to Asia and back to the west coast of the US. I know that the earth is round.

You are really not going to like what I have to say next.

I already don't like what you just said right there!

Let me tell you a little story. Once upon a time, there was a little boy who fell down a deep, dried-out well. Looking up, he could see a small round patch of blue sky.

And over time he began to think that the small patch of blue sky was all there was to the outside world, but he was wrong. Yes, I've heard this story before. My dad used to tell it to me all the time.

Sort of. Your dad would say that only a great fool looks up from the bottom of his particular well and thinks that patch of sky is everything there is of the outside world.

Same thing.

Yes, but let me tell you the rest of the story. To bide his time, the boy started changing the shape of the walls of the well. He would remove the stones from one area and add them to another. One day he made that well the shape of a plus sign, so the patch of sky looked like a plus sign instead of a circle.

Another time he made it in the shape of a triangle, so the sky looked like a triangle — and so on and so forth. He loved making new designs. Every day the sky looked different. Of course, the sky itself never really changed, just the shape of the well through which he was observing it. Do you see where I am going with this?

Are you going to tell me that my neural pathways are like the different shapes of that well?

Sort of. But that would be more like placing strands of yarn all up and down the well walls, crisscrossing each other and making a unique design that filters the light coming from above. But the point I really want to make is that what you perceive as the sky and the walls and the stones and the well itself — that is all determined by your physical senses. The sky is not really blue, even though all of you would see it that way. The reason you see it that way is because your eyes have a certain number of rods and cones, and the light that comes in through those rods and cones takes on a certain color that is associated with the wavelength of light that is being filtered through your eyes. But the sky is not really blue. It only looks like that because of the way the human eye has evolved.

The sky is not really blue?

No. Color does not really exist in the outside world. It is a subjective experience.

Is that true?

Of course, it is true. Imagine that you are standing in front of a beautiful pine tree. On your right shoulder is a bat. On your left shoulder is a live shrimp that you have in a jar of ocean water. At your feet is a snake. You are all facing the pine tree. But you are all experiencing something completely different.

How different?

You are experiencing the photons that bounce off of the tree and hit your eyes, with your three human photoreceptors, so you see a mix of green and brown. The shrimp, however, has fifteen photoreceptors, so the colors it is seeing through its eyes you can't even begin to imagine. The bat is creating an image of the tree in its mind based on sound waves that bounce off of the tree. The snake is creating an image of the tree in its brain based on thermal signatures from the tree. Do you have any frame of reference at all for what it would be like to create an image in your mind based on either sound or bio-thermal fluctuations?

There are so many different ways of perceiving the world around you. All you know is the human way. But guess what? Trees are also aware of the world around them. So are mushrooms. They communicate with each other across massive mycelia networks that function very similarly to the synaptic firing of your brain. Nature is full of different ways of perceiving the world. There are eight-billion different species of life on this planet, which means that there have evolved eight-billion different ways to perceive reality. Which one of those is the one true objective, universally correct way to perceive it?

What does his have to do with flat earthers? You aren't going to tell me that they evolved to see the world as flat instead of round, are you?

In a way, that is exactly what I am telling you. There is a very im-

portant human tendency called confirmation bias. Do you know what that is?

Of course, I do. It is the reason why people see what they want to see and believe what they want to believe.

And why people tend to turn a blind eye to evidence that would disprove something that they want to believe in. Confirmation bias has a similar effect on the way people perceive the world as the different sensory organs in the snake, human, butterfly, and shrimp. If you were able to somehow borrow the snake's thermal sensing system, you would understand why it experiences the pine tree as something completely different than you experience.

The same could be said if you put yourself into the figurative shoes of the flat earthers. They have legitimate reasons for believing what they believe, and for seeing what they see, and those subjective reasons are different from your subjective reasons for seeing what you see. But that does not make you right and them wrong.

But the earth is round, not flat!

That is correct, but it is only round because of the way your physical senses experience it.

Wait! Don't get all crazy on me here. The earth is round, period.

Try to listen to what I am about to tell you. I'm going to drop some science on you. Are you ready?

Do I want to be?

Of course, you do. You are the one in control, remember? I'm just your imagination, pushing you through all of this.

Fine. Go ahead. Drop your science on me.

With pleasure. When you learned physics in high school, you were taught a very common fiction. You were taught that electrons and protons are like tiny little separate billiard balls that spin around each other, like planets in a solar system, and that activity is what creates atoms. But that is not the actual truth.

It's not? What is the actual truth?

The actual truth is that every electron in your body is connected to every other electron that exists everywhere in this universe. They are not separate billiard balls spinning around other separate billiard balls. The electron is a quantum-ized bundle of energy from a massive electron energy field that fills the entire universe.

Is this another one of your fictions?

Yes, of course. But it is based on the most current, peer-reviewed scientific understanding that you currently have. But think about what that means. It means that everyone and everything is, quite literally, connected to everything else. We are all made from the same ener-

gy stuff, and that energy stuff is not really trillions of tiny separate things. The energy stuff is a single massive energy field. Everything is this massive energy field. There is no beginning to it. There is no end of it. It is all connected at the deepest energetic level. It is all one thing, but you do not perceive it that way. Why?

I don't know. Because it is too small?

Partly. But the real reason is that your physical senses, which are made from this energy stuff, have not evolved to detect it in any way. Your physical senses evolved to focus on very narrow spectrums of light and sound and smell and touch. You evolved to be repelled by the electromagnetic force that holds molecules together — the force that keeps you from falling through your chair every time you sit down, even though your chair is made up of mostly empty space — as are you, by the way.

But imagine if you had evolved to sense the electron field that fills the entire universe. Would a pine tree still look the same to you as it does now? If you were able to see the massive energy field, how would you know where the pine tree stopped and the air around it began? It would all look like what it is – a massive sea of energy. If you had evolved to sense all of this, would you experience space and time the same way that you do now? Would the planet earth still look round to you, or would you see it as it actually is: a single field of energy that fills up everything.

There are so many different ways of perceiving reality. Which one is the one true objective, universally correct way to perceive it? Every point of perception has its limitations, its blind spots. Only one point of perception encompasses everything there is to perceive, and that is what you would call God: the one consciousness that is the cumulation of all of the infinitely expanding perspectives in everything that exists — because it is the Source of all the infinitely expanding perspectives that are perceiving what they are perceiving.

When I tell you that God is all around you and that God is everything, I do not mean that as a metaphor. The Source Energy that creates everything is intelligent and aware of everything it is and of everything it is doing. Always.

Nothing can be more than that. Everything else is less than that.

So that is what I mean when I say that everything is a fiction. Every point of perception (except for one) is incomplete and inaccurate to one degree or another — or, at least, it is inaccurate if you believe that one perspective gives you a complete picture of the world. And the human perspective has so many limitations and so many blind spots that to call anything Truth as opposed to a fiction is the highest form of comedy.

Well, I'm glad we could all entertain you.

I'm glad, too. But, let's be complete and accurate here: you do far more than entertain! We wouldn't want to be accused of spreading fictions!

I'm getting up now. This is driving me absolutely crazy.

You can pretend to leave if that floats your boat. But don't forget, we're always all connected. Of course, you can continue to ignore that if you like.

Now I know why ignorance is bliss.

5 DUMBO'S BLACK FEATHER

The very things that held you down
are gonna carry you up and up and up.
— *Timothy Q. Mouse*

Hello? Quad? Are you there?

Yes. I am always here.

I need your help.

You always have it.

I'm serious, though. Can you be more than just my divine imagination for a minute? I'm really struggling here.

I know you are. I feel it, too. And like I said, I'm right here in it with you. What can I do to help?

I want to stop feeling like this.

You're a little discouraged right now, aren't you? I want you to stop feeling like this, too.

That isn't very helpful.

Me wanting the same thing that you want isn't very helpful?

Maybe it's just the way you said it. It doesn't feel very empathetic.

What does it feel like?

Dismissive. Uncaring. Judgmental.

Really? So, you feel like I am judging you for feeling discouraged?

Sorta, I guess.

But if you accept that I am your imagination, you realize that me judging you is the same thing as you judging yourself, right?

Yes. But that's not particularly helpful, either.

Because then you start judging yourself for judging yourself?

Exactly.

Vicious circle.

Tell me about it.

It's kind of like that for everything though, isn't it?

What do you mean?

Well, you are always looking out at the world from the bottom of your own particular well, so you are really only ever experiencing what the shape of your well walls is allowing you to see.

So even when you are having the best communication that you can possibly have with another person, you still don't really know exactly what they are saying or why they are saying it. You don't know if they mean something slightly different with the words than are using, or if they are being honest with you or not, or if they have ulterior motives — so you always have to use your imagination to one degree or another to fill in the gaps of what you don't know.

I guess.

Yes, you do. All the time. So, in that sense, you are always responding to what it is that you imagine. Which means that you are always in a very important dialogue with yourself — with your own imagination — whether you are aware of it or not.

Is this supposed to be helping me?

Do you want it to help you?

I just want to stop feeling so discouraged. I have been up all night replaying the same things in my head over and over again, and I just want it to stop.

So why bring this to me? What do you want me to do about it?

A miracle would be nice.

Ooooh! Miracles are my specialty! The best miracles are simply a change in your own perspective, you know. So, what kind of miracle are you looking for?

Well, I think we have established that you are the part of me that imagines the unimaginable. You are like the Starship Enterprise from *Star Trek*, boldly going where my understanding has never gone before.

That's a good way of looking at it.

So, I want to go where I currently am not. I called on you to help me climb out of this pit of despair.

From Star Trek to The Princess Bride. You are mixing your movie metaphors.

It's just how I feel. I haven't been able to get out of this funk on my own, which means that all the normal, regular things I usually do are not working. So I'm asking you to give me a supercharged boost of abnormal irregularity. Show me what

I haven't been able to see. Whatever I need to get me out of this pit.

With pleasure. So, your pit of despair, do you know what it is all about? What exactly are you feeling?

I'm feeling discouraged. Sad.

When did you start feeling this way?

I don't know.

Well, give it some thought. Your inner emotions are closely connected to the thoughts that you think. What thoughts have you been thinking recently?

I've been thinking about my past — things around my career, things involving various relationships, different opportunities I previously had but don't have any more. I have been thinking about failure and inadequacy, mostly. Do you want me to go into specifics?

Do you want to go into specifics?

Not really. That's what I have been doing over and over in my head since late last night. I think those specifics are making it harder to climb out of this pit.

I think you are right. Do you know why?

My guess is that I only have a certain amount of energy to focus with, and if I focus on the negative stuff, then I don't have any room for the positive stuff.

Pretty good. Why do you think you are doing that?

I don't know. I'm trying to stop, but I can't help it.

Sort of like a drug addiction maybe?

Maybe. But why would I be doing that to myself?

Old habits, probably. Sort of like worshipping your failures.

Worshipping my failures? That doesn't feel right. What do you mean by worship?

I mean worship like you would at church: focusing your thoughts on certain things that take a higher priority in your mind than other things that you could be thinking about instead. You always have choices about where you focus your attention, even when it feels like you don't. Focusing your attention on your thoughts is like watering a plant — keeping it alive; making it grow. What is that if not worship?

I guess. But worship makes it sound like I *want* these thoughts to grow.

Maybe you do. Maybe thinking that you are a failure is actually how you want to think of yourself. Maybe that's what we need to figure out.

This sounds like gaslighting and victim blaming, telling me that it's my fault for feeling discouraged. That isn't making me feel any better. Why would I do that to myself? It has to be something else.

Who else could be doing it? No one is telling you that you are a failure, are they? You are doing it all yourself. Why? Why are you focusing on your failures?

Because I don't like the fact that I failed, and I want to make sure I don't fail again.

At anything? Ever?

Yeah. I don't want to be a failure.

No one does. And in truth, no one is. Everyone is a success. Failing at something doesn't make you a FAILURE any more than stepping on a bug makes you a murderer. That's called labeling, and you want to be really careful of putting labels on things. Especially on yourself!

But I really have failed at things.

Of course, you have. Everyone fails at things. It is normal and natural and unavoidable. Sorry to break it to you, but you will fail again — frequently.

But to put this in a better perspective, you have succeeded at more things than you have failed at. Many more things. Things that you take for granted because you are so good at succeeding at them that you don't even give them a second thought.

That would be nice if it were true.

But it IS true! Do you know how many things you do on a day-to-day basis that are successful? Every time you take a breath, your body gets the oxygen it needs for success. Every time you have something to eat, you are successfully providing nourishment to your cells. Every thought you think is a successful act of creation, regardless of what that thought is.

Come on. You could say that about anyone. That's not the way people measure success.

Of course, we could say it about everyone. In fact, I think I did when I said, "everyone is a success." No one is a FAILURE even though everybody fails. You are making yourself feel bad because you are focusing on things that you judge as negative while you are simultaneously discounting things you do that are vitally positive to your very survival. And you are exaggerating what you see as failures to eclipse what you aren't recognizing or appreciating as successes.

You are blaming my depression all on me again, and it still isn't helping.

Please remember this: You are a collection of trillions and trillions of subatomic vibrations (a.k.a. Source Energy) deep inside of your body that are cooperating together to create all the necessary things that give you life. If those things were not successful, you would not be able to imagine yourself either in to or out of a pit of despair. Do you accept that?

> I guess. But it still doesn't change how I feel about the choices I have made with the life that Source Energy is providing me.

Do you accept that you are the energy that creates universes?

> I don't usually think of myself that way and I don't really know what that completely means, but okay, if you are talking about the atoms in my body, then yes, I accept that.

What it means is that the energy that creates universes flows through you and is the foundation of everything that you create as well.

> That just makes me feel even more guilty about using that Source Energy to create failures.

But from the point of view of Source Energy, your failures are not failures. Source Energy only wants experience. That's it. It doesn't matter to Source Energy what that experience is. Every experience becomes a significantly insignificant piece of the whole. Failures and successes alike are valid, worthy experiences. Source loves them all. And you would be better off if you could learn to love them, too.

All experiences are valid and worthy? *All* of them?

If all of your various experiences were not worth the effort of creating them, Source Energy would not continue to create them.

I'm not so sure about that, but again, this is not helping me feel any better about my career and relationship failures that put me in this pit of despair in the first place. I can't stop thinking about them.

And that is what is creating your despair. Fixating on those specific so-called failures is like decorating that pit to make it more comfortable to live in. It's like meticulously hand-painting little pity tiles, in high-def clarity with excruciating detail, depicting all the scenes from all the self-selected fictions that tell the story of your failure and your victimhood. You cannot imagine anything outside of that pit when you are so intently focused on the specific reasons why you feel like you belong in that pit — especially after spending so much time decorating it and worshipping it like you have.

I sort of know that already, but it doesn't really help me stop doing it. I still haven't been able to just move on.

Why not?

It feels irresponsible.

Irresponsible in what way?

Because I don't want to fail again like I have in the past. I can't just wish my failures away as if they never happened. These are legitimate concerns that I have.

Oooh! They are legitimate, huh? Worthy of worship and adoration, are they?

Don't make fun of me. If I just decide to ignore what I did because it makes me feel uncomfortable, then I will never address what needs to be addressed or fix what needs to be fixed.

So, you are in need of fixing, are you?

Everybody is to one degree or another.

Ouch! Is that really the hill you want to die on?

What do you mean?

I mean that every single person is a unique work of art with intrinsic value, and everyone is in a constant state of growth and change. No one ever has — or ever will — think, feel, or experience exactly what you think, feel, and experience. These differences are our greatest strengths. Judging those differences as bad or wrong, or labeling them as "failures" only separates you from feeling love and gratitude for your own unique life. No one needs fixing. No one is broken. You are the energy that creates universes creating something new and unique that never has — and never will — be created in exactly the same way ever again. That makes you precious: rare, not broken.

> That sounds good and all, but that is actually one of my main worries — that if I put on these rose-colored glasses and think that everything is just hunky dory and that nothing needs to be fixed then I will just be fooling myself.

Let me see if I understand this. It worries you to think that you and everyone else are already perfect just as you are — that no one is in need of fixing?

> Yes. I worry that this is just a made-up fiction that will keep me from seeing the truth.

Okay then. Get out your painting supplies. Let's meticulously decorate another pity tile for your pit.

> See, once again — super dismissive! I don't want to be dismissive of legitimate concerns. Empathy is important. Especially self-empathy.

So, let me see if I understand: You worry that if you truly accept yourself and love yourself for exactly who you are, so-called failures and all, without judgment, that you would be foolish. You worry that you would be lying to yourself if you don't see yourself as a failure because of things you have failed at. You worry that hiding your failures under a blanket of inflated and exaggerated successes would be dismissive and callous and perpetuate your patterns of failure.

Is that right?

Yes. Exactly.

Well, I think we have figured out now why you want to feel like a failure, then. You think you would be dishonest if you didn't, and you don't want to be dishonest — even though hiding your successes under a blanket of inflated and exaggerated failures doesn't seem to be nearly as dishonest to you.

Wait. Say that again.

You value honesty. You don't want to be dishonest. You think it would be dishonest to focus on positive things rather than focusing on the negative things. So, you ignore the positive and over-inflate the negative. I'm telling you that that is also dishonest. So, you really aren't avoiding dishonesty!

Great, so I'm failing at that, too. Thanks a lot.

I told you that failure was unavoidable and that you would do it again. Why not learn to find the good in it and turn towards gratitude for the things that you learn from your failures?

I guess, but I don't know how to do that. With everything we have talked about regarding the severe limits of human perception, the severe limits of human understanding, and the unavoidable role that imagination plays in filling in the gaps of what we don't really know — it just feels like a recipe for continued self-deception.

And so, what if it is?

That feels really bleak and hopeless.

Why?

Because it means I will always be deceiving myself.

What if you take out the word "deceive?" There is a lot of negative emotion around that word. How else could you express that idea without poisoning the well by baking negativity right into it?

I guess I could say that I am always creating fictions about what is real.

Even the word "fiction" has pretty negative implications, as we have seen. It makes it seem to you like your perspective is invalid or unreal. Try again.

I can't think of anything else. Can't you just tell me a better word to use?

It will be more effective if it comes directly from you rather than indirectly through me.

But you are my imagination, right? Aren't I simply asking my imagination to show me a healthier way of looking at this?

You tell me.

I'd rather *you* told *me.*

I'm sure you would. So, pretend that you are me. That shouldn't be too hard, should it? What would you tell me? What's the first thing that pops into your head?

Well, I guess it's sort of like Dumbo's black feather.

Interesting. In what way?

Dumbo the elephant was born with abnormally large ears. It made him different from other elephants, and that difference put him in his own pit of despair. But those ears also gave him the ability to fly. He just didn't know it. Not until he got that magical black feather.

And what was magical about the black feather?

Nothing, really. It was a placebo. It only had as much power as Dumbo gave to it through his beliefs — how he imagined it. But it was just a normal black feather.

How did he get the black feather?

He got drunk one night and flew up into a tree. When he sobered up, he was terrified. How did he get in that tree? His little mouse friend told him that he flew up on his own power, but Dumbo didn't believe him. So, the mouse plucked a feather from a nearby crow and told Dumbo that it was magic and that the magic made him fly. And it worked! If Dumbo held onto that black feather, he was able to fly.

So, are you like Dumbo and I am like your little mouse friend?

I guess. But the point is that Dumbo didn't really need that black feather. It wasn't really magic. That was a fiction.

An effective fiction.

Yes, but Dumbo built his confidence on that fiction. So when the black feather was gone, he thought his own power to fly was gone, too.

I see. So, Dumbo crashed to the ground and died — big time elephant failure. The end?

No, he figured out at the last minute that the power was within himself the whole time.

Interesting. So, what is the power that is within you and what are your black feathers?

I'm not sure what power is within me, but the black feathers are all of the fictions that I tell myself.

All of them? Don't some of your fictions act more like rusty chains, holding you to the ground rather than inspiring you to fly?

I suppose.

So not all fictions are equal?

I guess not, but if what you are saying is right — that we really aren't ever able to perceive and understand the whole truth of anything — then fictions are pretty much all we have, and that is just super discouraging.

Why is it discouraging?

Because if everything is a fiction, then nothing is real!

That is all-or-nothing thinking. Reality includes everything that exists, right?

Of course.

And a story that you make up that is based on real things that you really experience and understand — even if you only experience and understand part of what really happened — that is all a part of reality, right?

But if I am believing lies — things that don't really exist even if I think they do — and if I can never really know the difference between lies and truth, then what is the point?

Ah, I see. So, you are feeling nihilistic, like there is no truth, like it's all lies, so what's the point?

Isn't that what I just said?

Sure, but you also just told me about Dumbo's black feather. You also just acknowledged that some fictions can help you unlock power that was inside you the whole time, power that you just couldn't accept any other way (because, by default, you believed a fiction that made you believe that you have no special power).

So, why ask, "What is the point?" Don't you see the point? Don't you see that if you are the intentional author of your own fictions, that you can take control of the fictions in your life and create more black feathers that unlock hidden truths instead of rusty chains that hold you down?

But that still feels fake.

What does "fake" mean? You said that Dumbo didn't really need his black feather, but he sort of did, didn't he? He didn't go from self-doubt to self-acceptance without it. So even though it was a "fake" fiction, it was a valuable "fake" fiction, right?

Yes.

So why not become a more intentional author of your own valuable fictions. Why not use them to chip away at the limiting fictions? You are already the one authoring all of your fictions anyway. You are the one focusing on your so-called failures rather than acknowledging your multiple effortless successes — both of which are equally valid and real. Why are you focusing on only a small part of what is true and ignoring the rest? What if you started being more picky about the stories you tell yourself? What if you started being more intentional about the mosaics that you paint on your tiles?

That sounds easier said than done.

Maybe to start out with. Especially if you have developed a habit of self-sabotage through your own thoughts. But isn't it at least worth a try?

It still feels fake.

Because you are not used to it. But if you take the time to really be honest with yourself, don't you recognize that the story you are telling yourself about being a failure is also fake? It is incomplete. It is exaggerated.

Wait. The things I failed at are real! They are not fake!

The things that happened that you are calling failures are real things, but they are only "failures" because you are calling them that and because you are judging them by a very narrow, incomplete standard — which means that you are removing your successes from the scale and weighing only what you see as negative.

Try thinking about it this way: every experience you've ever had has brought you to exactly this point in time right now. And right now, you are alive; you are safe; you are loved. That, in and of itself, is success — if you allow it to be. And that success is because of every-thing you have ever done — including the so-called failures.

See, you don't have to make up fake stories about things that nev-er actually happened to accomplish the miracle of changing your perspective; you just need to learn to be more true to your actual successes.

So, the way I have been looking at things is wrong, is it? That sounds like I am broken and need to be fixed, and you said earlier that no one is broken and no one needs to be fixed.

And you said that you didn't want to look at things the same way that you have always been looking at them. You wanted me to give you a "supercharged boost of abnormal irregularity," remember?

So, you can interpret what I told you to mean that you are broken and need to be fixed if you want to. There is nothing wrong with that.

Of course, you could also interpret it to mean that your awareness of who you are and all the ways that you are NOT BROKEN is expand-ing — and that may be a more effective interpretation in helping you change your mood.

I guess. It still just seems a little hard to wrap my head around.

Didn't you ask me to help you see another perspective? Why are you fighting it? Don't you want to give it an honest shot and see for yourself if this will help you feel better?

Of course. So how do I do it?

Exactly how you are doing it now. You have a desire to get out of the pit of despair. Follow that desire. Imagine what it feels like to be out of the pit. Do it right now. How would you feel if you weren't feeling so discouraged?

I would feel better.

In what ways?

I would be smiling instead of scowling.

Good. So, make yourself smile instead of scowl. Create that feeling for yourself right now.

But that's just faking it.

You really can't get past this "faking" thing, can you? OK, let's try something to make this a little more real. I want you to try to understand the way all of these thoughts exist inside of your brain: as real, actual, physical, observable, powerful, impactful, measurable things.

Close your eyes and try to imagine what the inside of your brain looks like. Imagine a web of neural connections, dark grey matter, folds upon folds of spiderweb-like synaptic connections. Can you picture it?

Sort of.

Now add an electrical storm to it. Imagine flashes of energy, like lightening, flashing on and off in random order all across this webbed network. Can you picture that?

Yes.

Each flash of light is intelligence being communicated from one part of your body to another, and the order of those flashes correspond to specific actions that your body takes.

Want to see what this looks like from the inside? In your mind's eye, raise your right hand above your head and watch the neural activity that monitors, regulates, and controls that action. Can you see it?

I can sort of picture what you are describing.

Good. Now do the same thing for your left hand and pay attention to the flashes. Can you see a difference?

Well, obviously I can't really see what is going on, but I get your point. There must be differences in the neural activity between moving my right hand vs. moving my left hand.

Can you imagine what those flashes would look like if you moved your foot instead of your hand?

I can try.

What about the flashes that tell you that you are hungry? Or cold? What do they look like?

I don't really know. But again, I assume they look different. This is getting tedious. What are you getting at?

From a neurological perspective, these flashes — these synaptic firings — are all real. They are not fake. They happen. And your body has a real response when they do. From that perspective, does it really matter if you are raising your arm in response to something that is "really" there or not? Your brain activity is real. The impact on your body is real.

And this is helping me how?

You said that you would be faking it if you smiled instead of scowled. My question is, from the perspective of brain activity, what exactly is being faked?

If I'm feeling discouraged, but I'm pretending not to be discouraged, isn't that fake?

But you said that you want that feeling to go away. You desire to feel differently. Is that desire real or is that desire fake?

I just worry that I might be suppressing real feelings that could get stuck in my body and create problems for me later on.

And how is all that worrying working out for you?

I hope that it keeps me honest.

You are afraid you are not being honest?

I just want to be sure.

I thought that you wanted a miracle.

I do.

And what miracle is that? To feel good when you aren't feeling good? To be real when you worry that you are being fake?

You're making it sound stupid.

I don't think it's stupid at all. I think it is very natural. Very normal. Very human. You want the greatest miracle in the history of miracles. You want a change in your own perspective. You want the power to choose self-love even when immersed in a sea of fear and self-doubt. That is not stupid. That is wise. Especially when you learn how to actually do it.

So how do I do it?

Just like you are doing it right now.

And how is that?

You turned inward. You asked for help. You confronted your feelings. You felt them. You acknowledged and respected them. Then you reframed them. You reminded yourself that there are other ways of seeing this: more neutral ways, more accepting ways, more reasonable ways, more loving ways. You intentionally shaped your thoughts to take you out of a pit of despair towards an ocean of peace and gratitude.

This, by the way, is your special inner power — your own Dumbo-like ability to fly. This is the power of that electrical storm in your mind. What you think impacts how you feel. If you can train yourself to be grateful for every synaptic spark, without judging whether it was right or wrong, real or fake — that's your black feather. And you are doing it right now. It is working. Am I right? Don't you feel better now than you did when we started?

I think so. But how can I know for sure? How do I know I'm not just fooling myself?

As opposed to how you were fooling yourself by labeling yourself a failure? You want to know the truth? You are always fooling yourself! All of your stories are fictions! You never have the whole picture of anything. You are always making guesses and filling in details to compensate for missing data. Always. You can't get away from that. So, take control of it by intentionally shaping your

thoughts to match the emotions you want to feel! Perfect that power-
er of yours. Then you will know for sure that you are giving life
your very best shot, and that best shot is yours. You are in control
of where you aim and how and when you shoot. Always. Whether
you are aware of it or not.

And remember, from the point of view of brain activity, no shot is
ever wrong. Your shot may not go in the hoop, to use a basketball
reference. It may clang off the rim. It may be a total air ball. But a
successful shot — from the perspective of brain activity — is any
shot where brain activity is present. That is a valid measure of
success.

Of course, the more you practice and fine-tune your skills to hit
the targets that you aim for, the more effective your shot will be,
and that is another valid measure for another kind of success. But
shooting and missing is never, ever wrong. And the fine-tuning and
adjusting of your thoughts is never, ever finished. Does that make
sense?

I guess.

So how do you feel now?

Better.

Are you still in the pit?

Not so much.

Has your perspective shifted?

I think. A little.

Fantastic. Another miracle.

Thank you.

You are welcome.

6 SCIENCE AND SKEPTICS AND ONIONS (OH MY!)

> Doubt is an uncomfortable condition,
> but certainty is a ridiculous one.
> — *Voltaire*

Hey buddy, do you have a minute?

Sure Quad. Nice that you are contacting me this time.

I am always contacting you. Nice of you to actually respond to me this time.

Fair enough. What's up?

I composed a song for you about science and skeptics and onions. Want to hear it?

A song?

Yes. Here are the words. Figure out the music on your own:

Think about this carefully, and think about it now.

Do we know more about the world today than we did 100 years ago? How about 10 years ago? One year ago?

Scientific understanding continues to increase. Hooray for science! Technology, understanding, progress. We love science!

But here is the question I sing to your soul:

What great understanding are we all increasing towards? What will be the last thing we discover? What will be the end result? Will there ever come a day when all that there is to discover will be discovered?

Once upon a time, a human child was born into a small wandering tribe of hunter gatherers. For a time, they thought their tribe was the only tribe out there. Eventually, however, they discovered that there were other tribes, other people. Different tribes, different people, different languages, different customs. Some of them friendly, some of them threatening. Some tribes completely destroyed other tribes. Some tribes put their differences aside and joined together to create a larger tribe, larger customs, larger and more unified perspectives. From many small groups to fewer large ones.

Are we moving towards a day when all such separateness is obliterated?

Are we moving towards a day when all that exists is seen to fit seamlessly together as one amazing whole?

Is that knowledge already out there, just waiting to be discovered?

Did Antarctica exist before it was discovered?

What was the tallest mountain in the world before Everest was dis-covered? Wasn't it still Everest, whether anyone knew it yet or not?

When all of the land masses on this planet have been explored, and all of their hidden secrets have been revealed — when the depths of the ocean have been visited and studied to the very core of this earth — when every planet in this solar system has been equally explored and studied and documented — when other solar systems and galaxies have been explored, will there still be other univers-es to explore — other ways that existence is organized that go on forever?

When every cell and molecule and atom has been explored, and ev-ery quark and subatomic particle of fundamental energy been fully identified and understood for what it is and what it does — when the mystery of dark matter has been solved — when a unified theory of everything leaves no further questions about quantum mechanics and the theory of relativity — when each layer of the onion has been peeled away, will we ever find a definite center? Or will we simply find more mysterious layers upon layers of fundamental energetic onionistic existence?

What is the one unifying truth that already exists that we simply have yet to discover?

Is there one unifying truth, or are we making all of this up as we go along?

How can we even know?

If we have always discovered that we are constantly receiving new information that requires us to update and adjust our current understanding — if we have always discovered that there is always more to discover — if there has always been something else just on the other side of the limits of our perception, then what makes us so certain that there is a single constant universal Truth that will one day be discovered? What evidence supports that assumption at all?

What makes us think that the very act of exploration and discovery is not fundamentally — in and of itself — an act of creation that alters the very system that it is exploring? What makes us so certain that our ever-changing understanding is not creating biases that influence not only the types of questions that we will ask, but also the types of answers that we accept? What makes us think that new questions and mysteries and possibilities are not constantly emerging simply because of our own desire to discover them — our own insatiable thirst for more mysteries to solve? Where is the evidence to support the belief that one day we will figure it all out, and that we are constantly progressing closer and closer to the day when everything there is to know is known?

What makes the self-proclaimed skeptic believe that he is a skeptic when he holds steadfast to rigid assumptions and refuses to engage in genuine searches for greater understanding; when he refuses to

entertain ideas that he deems as "impossible" and will not even ex-
amine the evidence (or lack of evidence) that supports his particular
degree of certainty?

When will we glimpse the Everest that has always been our ulti-
mate truth: that existence is infinite, omniscient, omnipotent, ever
growing, ever evolving? That imagination pushes the limits of our
ever-expanding perceptions?

That what we call life and death is but one variation of an infinitely
expanding unfolding of possibilities?

That our malleable reality is nothing more than a temporary snap-
shot of the limits of our perception?

Where are the egg men?
Where is the Walrus?
Koo koo kachoob.

That's it. What do you think?

You call that a song?

What would you rather have me call it: a lobster?

You are really weird.

There is certainly plenty of evidence for that!

7 GOOD VIBRATIONS

I'm pickin' up good vibrations
She's giving me excitations
(ooom bop bop)
— *Brian Wilson of The Beach Boys*

Hey Quad, I've got something I want to ask you about.

What is it?

I want to better understand what people mean when they talk about energy and vibrations.

All people? Everyone means something a little different, you know.

Well, I guess I want to better understand energy and vibrations in general.

What do you want to better understand about them?

Well, it sounds pretty kooky to me, honestly, when I hear

people say that we have to align our vibrations to this thing or that thing. I guess I want to know if there is really anything to it, or if it is just a bunch of gobbledygook.

OK, got it. Where do you want me to start?

Where do you want to start?

Let's start with you. With who you are — and what you are — right here in this specific place and time.

OK, that seems easy enough.

I want to take a kind of mental snapshot — a single moment in time — like a photograph, or a single frame in a strip of movie film. So describe to me right now where you are and what you are doing.

I am at home, in my bathroom, stretched out in a warm bath, typing this on my phone early in the morning.

Is there daylight outside? Has the sun come up yet?

Yes. The sun is just now rising.

Are there birds flying around?

I can hear birds outside my window.

So, this is our snapshot: you in the bathtub writing this out on your phone while the sun is rising outside and birds are singing. Of course, a lot of other things are going on right now as well, but everything is frozen in place for a split second in this snapshot of time. Can you picture it?

Yes.

So, in that snapshot, are there any vibrations going on around you?

I don't think so. Vibrations require movement, don't they? And this is a static snapshot of time.

Good. So, move the snapshot forward a frame or two, like you would with a strip of movie film. You should see a bit of movement. Do you see any vibrations now?

Vibrations of what?

Of anything. Light. Sound. Water. Is anything vibrating that you can tell?

I don't know. This is getting a little weird for me. Maybe I don't want to do this after all.

We can stop anytime you want to, but let me just paint this picture for you, because this is what you really want to know:

Right now, you are surrounded by electromagnetic waves, which includes what you recognize as visible light, as well as invisible infra-

red, microwave, UHF, VHF, shortwave, mediumwave, ultraviolet, gamma, X-rays, etc. etc. These are all constantly vibrating around you and through you. In fact, you are as immersed in those electromagnetic waves as you are in the water in your bathtub.

Some of those waves pass through your body. Some of them bounce off of your body. But they are constantly surrounding you. If you could actually see all of it, you wouldn't know what you were looking at.

If it's always around me, and constantly interacting with me, am I aware of any of it at all?

Of course ,you are. When any of these vibrating waves hit your eyes, your body instantly filters it and sends signals to your brain. A small percentage of it is recorded in your conscious awareness — what you are able to see. But most of it is recorded in your subconscious. For example, you can't see the ultra violet rays from the sun that give you a sunburn if you stay out in it too long, but your body is aware of what is going on, and the sunburn is the evidence that there is a real, measurable reaction to those invisible ultraviolet rays. It is a mistake to think that what you are consciously aware of is the only kind of awareness that you have. There is way more going on subconsciously that impacts the way you live your life. And believe it or not, you are vibration as well.

I am vibration? How does that work?

Every atom in your body is energy — little sparks of intelligent po-

tential that were baked in the stars. All that energy is moving, os-cillating, vibrating, and — sorry, this might freak you out a little bit — every bit of energy in your body is also constantly flickering on and off. This is relationship between matter and anti-matter. You don't register all this with your conscious awareness, of course, just like you don't register all the empty space that exists inside of each of your atoms. But try to imagine what you would see if your eyes were able to detect the swirling, vibrating, flickering collection of subatomic energy that you are. Not only is the world outside of you constantly vibrating, so is the world inside of you. And those vi-brations interact with and influence each other like ripples on the surface of your bath water. All. The. Time.

In fact, if you could see yourself through the eyes of Source Ener-gy, you would not recognize what you see at all. Every thought you think, every movement you make: all of it is vibrational waves of energy.

So, it's real? Energy and vibration? It's not just kooky New-Age mumbo jumbo?

Yes, it's real; and yes, it is also kooky New-Age mumbo jumbo. Just because you are made out of energy and vibration doesn't mean that you can control it to work magic — to enforce your will on the out-side universe. You are a small, significantly insignificant thing that this vibrational Source Energy is doing, and you are limited in what you are able to perceive and influence.

The real power that you have is over your own thoughts — and, more precisely, over opening or closing your heart to the world around you. In any moment you could choose to respond from a place of shame, guilt, grief, or apathy — desire, anger, pride, courage — neutrality, acceptance, willingness, reason, love, or peace. In fact, the main purpose of your life is to learn to channel your own internal vibrations — your thoughts and emotions — to move from the more negative, life-draining thoughts and emotions to the more positive, life-affirming thoughts and emotions. It is all energy. It is all vibration. And yes, it is also pretty kooky. But that just makes it all the more delicious.

Delicious?

Trust me. It's an acquired taste.

8 DO THOUGHTS CREATE REALITY?

Whether you think you can,
or think you cannot,
you're right.
— *Henry Ford*

The closer you come to knowing
that you alone create the world of your experience,
the more vital it becomes for you to discover
just who is doing the creating.
— *Eric Michael Leventhal*

I'm back for more.

That was quick.

It's getting more fun.

I know right?

So, here is what I want to know today. I hear people talking about the power of our thoughts — they say that thoughts create reality. Part of me really understands and accepts this idea as rational, practical, and naturalistic — all actions begin in the mind as either conscious or unconscious thoughts. But there is also part of me that is super resistant to the magical-thinking part of this idea: where people say that all you have to do is think something to make it come true — as if I could just imagine myself having a million dollars and then all of a sudden I come across million dollars. So, I want to hear from you, my imagination, who should have a pretty good grasp on the world of thoughts. Do thoughts actually create reality?

This is one of my favorite subjects to talk about. The short answer is yes. But to really understand it, you first need to understand what thoughts are, what reality is, and the overall process of turning thoughts into things — which they already are, of course, even if you don't think of them that way. Thoughts themselves are real physical electromagnetic things that flash on and off for a time in your brain. And the growth of a thought is an evolution; it functions a lot like ... well ... evolution. So that's where I want to start.

You want to start with evolution?

It's as good a place as any. What are your thoughts on evolution? Do you believe that humans evolved from apes?

Funny. No, humans did not evolve from apes. Both humans and apes evolved from a common ancestor, but whatever that was, it was neither human nor ape. Not yet.

That's right. I was testing you. You passed. And what was that com-

mon ancestor before it was your common ancestor?

Another common ancestor, I guess. A whole series of them, each one less and less complex the further back you go until you get to the original single-celled life form on this planet from which all life is descended.

You are mostly right about that. Things don't always evolve from less complex to more complex. Sometimes things evolve to become more efficient, but less complex — some of their biological systems adapt to better survive in the environment of the time. And the idea that there was — once upon a time — just one single-celled organism from which everything evolved is also a bit too simple.

There were — and still are — multiple single-celled organisms that live and die and compete for resources and influence other forms of life around them — sometimes forming symbiotic relationships with other life forms and eventually evolving into a single life form. That has happened with your species a number of times and will continue to occur far into the future. But basically, your understanding of evolution is correct.

Life changes over time. It adapts to its environment. It responds to hostility and conflict. Many forms of life adapt to new environmental changes and thrive. Many more do not, and instead become fuel for those that do. In this sense, all forms of life cooperate together — you know, pushing, pulling, and contributing to a larger living ecosystem. And this process doesn't happen overnight. It takes time. At least in those dimensions where space-

time is built into the fabric of reality.

Okay, that is cool and all, but what does it have to do with thoughts?

Thoughts evolve in a similar way.

How?

What does life need to grow? It needs to be nurtured; it needs to be fed; it needs an environment that supports its growth; it needs to reproduce. The most successful forms of life find a way to survive at least long enough to create a duplicate of themselves, and those duplicates are mostly exact replications, with minor variations that pop up here and there.

But, over time, those minor variations eventually create new forms and species of life. And the most robust forms of life adopt traits that allow them to survive in the most hostile environmental conditions. And so it is with thoughts. You feed them. You keep them alive by the focus of attention you give them. You provide an environment where they thrive. They reproduce new thoughts and they slowly change over time. And they grow. Some thoughts really take on a life of their own. Do you see the similarities?

I guess. But thoughts are just thoughts. They just exist in our minds. They aren't really like living things that exist in the outside world.

What is inside and what is outside? That is only a statement of per-spective. What is inside of your head is outside of someone else's. And what is inside of their head is outside of your own. But those thoughts are, in fact, physical, measurable things that exist in the world, regardless of inside or outside.

But I don't ever see my thoughts.

Or hear, or smell, or feel them. Yes, I know. But you could see them with the right equipment. Thoughts are very real. Think of them as the tiny bolts of lightning that make up the immense electrical storm of your mind. Some thoughts you create all by yourself. Many thoughts you acquire from others. The origin of thoughts is a fas-cinating conversation all its own. But you want to know if thoughts create reality.

I'm telling you that thoughts already are reality. It's like asking if a single thread exists separate from the fabric you are observ-ing. It's like asking if a single thread can create a fabric. The fab-ric is made of multiple threads just as reality is made of multiple thoughts. Thoughts behave very much like living things. They are like threads that can change their color, their size, and their tensile strength. Imagine a piece of fabric constructed of ever-changing strings of thread.

But thoughts aren't really threads, though. And reality is not really fabric. People say that their thoughts can make them prosperous and wealthy. That all we have to do to have a million dollars is to think about having a million dollars and then poof — magic, presto — there appears your million dollars, magically manifested by your thoughts.

Well, if that is how you are defining thoughts creating reality, then you have baked your answer right into the question. I'm talking to you about a process by which the thoughts you think shape and change the world in which you live.

But thoughts are just thoughts, and people think they can just make reality change through their thoughts.

And I am telling you they are right, even if the process they think is happening is not. But I see this is hard for you, so let's back up. Tell me what you mean by "thoughts."

You know ... thoughts, impulses, instincts, and the things we think. Like, "I'm hungry. I could really go for a corn dog." Or, "Look at how beautiful that woman is over there." Or, "Look at those birds sailing in the wind like that. I sure wish I could fly." You know, thoughts like that.

Where do those thoughts come from?

From my brain?

Where in your brain?

From neurons communicating with other neurons bio-chemically through synaptic gaps.

Look at you, Mr. Fancy Pants!

Yeah, I looked it up.

So, let's take one of those examples — the one about people watching birds and wishing that they could fly. Humans have been having those kinds of thoughts and hopes and wishes ever since they could look up and see birds flying above them. Have any of those thoughts become reality? Have any of those thoughts been nurtured and fed and grown to a point where humans can actually fly?

No. And we won't either. You don't just grow wings and feathers through wishful thinking.

Oh yes, "wishful thinking," the backhanded compliment from people too smart to be fooled by "wishful thinking." Well, what if we told you that the wishful (and courageous!) thinking of two brothers — Orville and Wilbur Wright — allowed mankind to take a major leap towards turning those age-old hopes and wishes into true actual reality?

But that's not the same thing.

Why not?

Because that is just technological progress. There isn't any biological change to the human form that allowed our skin to turn to feathers or our arms turn into wings.

Of course not. Who said that was going to happen?

You did when you brought up the example of evolution.

I used evolution as a metaphor to help you understand the process by which thoughts become things. There are many ways to evolve. You yourself mentioned technological progress. That's just another way of saying evolution of technology. And technology does not evolve by itself. It evolves through the careful focus and concentration of the human mind.

You are making a huge mistake if you overlook the evolution of the brain — the evolution of being able to comprehend what had previously been incomprehensible — to stretch, to grow, to adapt. That is what allows technological progress. That is how man turned his age-old desire to fly into a reality that has rapidly changed the world you live in.

But it's still not the same thing. That was done through technology. Not through nature.

Oh really? And what exactly is nature?

Nature is nature. Why do you ask such obvious questions?

To challenge your assumptions. You divide existence up into these funny categories like organic and inorganic, natural and unnatural. If I pointed out a bird's nest and asked you if it was natural or unnatural, you would say it is natural, because it is made out of twigs and leaves and other things that naturally grew out of nature. But it didn't grow naturally into the shape of the nest. Birds build it. Birds turned their own bird thoughts from their bird brains into bird realities. They thought, "I need something for warmth and security and shelter," and eventually they figured out how to gather bits of things to put together into the reality of, "Look, I built a nest."

Sure. And all of this is just part of nature.

Of course. And nature manipulating nature is still an example of nature. But let's say that the nest was made from twigs and leaves and some old shredded plastic bags and pieces of ribbon. What would you consider that?

Still pretty much nature probably.

What if the nest were made entirely of shredded plastic?

I don't know. It's still a nest built by a bird, so I'd still think of it as nature.

I would too. So why is that different from when a human builds an airplane? How is that not also an example of nature manipulating nature?

Because the materials of an airplane are a little different than the materials of the nest.

Sure, there are differences. But if you really break it down to the most fundamental nature of nature, everything is made from atoms — electrons, protons, and neutrons. If you look at it from that perspective, everything is part nature.

But these are man-made things. Not things that naturally grow in nature.

So, man is not an extension of nature? Man is something different?

No, but still ...

I understand that you think it is different. To prepare for death, you spend thousands of dollars on durable coffins to keep your corpse separate from the earth it came from. You think that nature is something you have to fight against, to conquer, to tame. But you are just as much the fruit of this planet as an apple is the fruit of a tree. And if an apple could manipulate the basic building blocks of nature to create metal things that fly in the air, wouldn't you consider that nature begetting more nature, just like when a bird builds a nest?

I'd consider that super weird. What is your overall point?

My overall point is that the human thought, "I wish I could fly," did, in fact, became a reality. Just like the thought, "I wish I could cure deadly diseases," or, "I wish that we could fly to the moon," or, "I wish that I could produce enough food to feed the entire world." But it doesn't happen overnight. It is a process that is very natural. And anything that is created from the human mind is an extension of human nature.

So, thoughts *do* create reality?

Yes, and in many more ways than what we have already described. You could also close your eyes and imagine yourself eating a cold, crispy, juicy apple, and the very thought of that imaginary apple would activate physical processes in your body that are similar to if you were actually eating an apple. You can almost taste it just by thinking of it. That doesn't mean that if you think of an apple, an apple will magically appear.

But that thought does make an impact on what you call reality. If you think anxious thoughts and worry a lot, your body creates excessive amount of cortisol, which impacts your overall health — another way that thoughts create reality. There is also this little thing called confirmation bias, which says that once you make up your mind about something, you easily find evidence to support your conclusions and become blind to any evidence to the contrary. But the most important way that thoughts create reality is the way that you train your brain to focus attention.

If you teach yourself that you are a victim all the time, you will see yourself as a victim all the time. If you train yourself to find something to be genuinely grateful for in every experience, you will find things to be genuinely grateful for in every experience. The thoughts you think have a profound impact on the way you see the world and on the way you see yourself in it.

Kind of like the thoughts that are inspiring me to write all of this right now?

Yes. Exactly like that. And if you want to go even deeper, ask me sometime about the way the thoughts you think in this form of life you are in right now become the fabric from which your future lives are formed. But don't ask me now. Take some time to understand and appreciate the thoughts you are having now. Appreciate them; feed them; watch them grow — and soon you will be hungry for more.

That has given me a lot to think about!

Just keeping it real.

9 ALL ABOUT SOULS

My soul is from elsewhere,
I'm sure of that,
and I intend to end up there.
— *Rumi*

I'm back.

I never left. You just stopped listening.

I didn't stop listening, *per se*. I just stopped asking for a while, cuz your answers were getting sorta lame.

Yes, I remember. So, you're back. What do you want?

I want to know what a soul is.

Why?

I don't know; I just do. I hear people talk about souls all the time, but it doesn't totally make sense to me.

How could it?

Wait ... you're turning this around on me already?

You are turning it around on yourself. You already know that there are severe limits to what you can know, and yet you keep wanting to know more, to understand better.

It's true. I want to know more. I want to understand better.

We know. It's cute. We really do love it.

We?

Yes. "We." This is why you want to know what a soul is, right? You want to know the rest of you. Of us. What we all are together.

Yeah, I guess.

Which is everything.

Everything?

And that includes us.

Well, I am making up this conversation with you in my head, so that makes sense that you would be at least be part of me.

Which sense?

What?

You said it makes sense that we would be a part of you. Which sense is it? Do you hear us? See us? Feel or taste or smell us?

No, I just think you. You are my imagination.

And which of those five senses is that?

I don't know ... touch maybe?

Why do you say that?

Because my thoughts are electrical currents or synapses or something like that in my brain.

And how is that touch? Can you feel it happening? Do you physically sense these electrical currents that you speak of?

Well, they are impacting and interacting with something in my brain, like a lightning storm, right? Lightning hits things.

Sure, but light photons impact and interact with your optic nerves, and you call that sight instead of touch. Sound waves impact and interact with your eardrum, and you call that sound instead of touch. Smells and tastes impact and interact with physical receptors on your nose and tongue, but you don't consider those as a sense of touch either.

Why are you derailing me? I want to know about souls.

We are derailing you to show you that your primary way of creating meaning in this world — your inner thoughts — (those many, many silent stories you tell yourself; the way that you perceive reality; that part of you where you spend most of your time and energy and focus) cannot be explained by any of the five senses. People use the idea of a "sixth sense" as a joke — as some kind of woo-woo meta-physical ESP — when, really, your imagination is your first sense. Imagination is more crucial to your perceived life experience than any of the five physical senses.

And this has to do with souls how?

Because unless we describe something to you that you can see, hear, taste, smell, or touch — or even imagine that you can — the words we use will be incomprehensible to you.

I hate it when you go there. It's such a cop-out! Yes, I get it. There are severe limitations on what I can comprehend. So, use your eternal infinite wisdom and brilliance to give me a metaphor, then, and just answer this question the best you can.

Fine. Tell us where you are confused.

Well ... I can accept that we are all made up of pure positive energy—atoms and electrons and quantum energy and all that. I understand that this energy that makes up who I am right now is indestructible eternal energy that is only on loan to me. This energy was something else before it was me.

We were many something elses before we were you (and even during, if you really want to go there).

And the energy will be something else after me.

We will be many something elses. Go on.

So, I get that. This energy that is me is also the air that I breathe and the ground that I stand on and everything in this world — living or otherwise. It is all this eternal cosmic energy.

You are preaching to the choir. We are that energy. All of us.

Right, sure. I mean, even if you are just synaptic electric lightning-storm thought-forms that I am manufacturing in my imagination, you are that same energy.

And so, your confusion?

So, what is a soul, then? If, when I die, I turn back into the pure positive energy that was part of the flowing fabric of everything that I was before I ever was, I don't see how each unique, individual person could have a unique, individual soul.

So, you are asking us if you have "a soul" that is distinct from some-one else's soul?

Yes. Like the way people talk about living past lives, or their soul coming into this lifetime with some kind of karmic debt to pay, or a "soul contract" that they have with another person. I don't know how that fits with the "we are all pure positive energy" thing.

And you want to know even though you know that you can't know. But you want some kind of metaphor to make you feel like you actually know what you know you totally can't know?

Exactly.

OK. We can appreciate that. But keep in mind, this metaphor is for you — because you asked, because of how you asked, and because of where you are in your ability and desire to comprehend beyond the limits of your personal comprehension (which is an ever-evolving compilation of every distinct experience you have experienced within your lifetime). This metaphor will make more sense to you than to anyone else, so don't think you are getting an answer for everyone. This is being delivered especially to you.

OK. That seemed a bit long and unnecessary.

Picture a wet floor in a locker room. Or maybe water spots on a window. Or drops of mercury on a cold metal plate. Whatever it is, imagine hundreds, thousands, or even billions of little droplets all coming into contact with each other, merging together as they touch, forming larger droplets, fewer of them but bigger, merging together, merging together — coming together based on their location and vibration and mood and so many other unifying or repelling factors — until the last biggest droplets overcome their resistance and merge with each other until there is just one. And then it shatters into hundreds of thousands of billions of droplets and goes through that entire process again. Can you picture that?

Yes. Is that a soul?

Yes and no; but mostly no. It's a process. It's a way for you to step outside of your human-formed conception of life and attempt to grasp what has been happening on this planet. You call her Mother Earth. She is your mother. This pure positive energy that you are made from is energy from this earth. The same energy that is rock and tree and bird and fish and insect and mushroom and plastic and glass and everything — everything on this planet. And the process of shattering into millions of pieces and coming back together happens many, many times at many, many levels of existence. It happens outside of and independent from your linear sense of space and time.

Are you saying that the earth is a soul and we are all pieces of that earth-soul that are merging back into each other?

Yes and no; but mostly no. I am painting a metaphorical picture to illustrate something that is far beyond the realm of your understanding. So, don't get too attached to the water droplets or the earth metaphor.

OK. But how does this help me with soul mates and soul contracts and past lives and karma and all that stuff?

Well, don't get attached to any of those metaphors, either. They each do a fine job of illustrating many peoples' perception of the process as they understand and experience it. But remember, these are all stories and symbols. None of them are anywhere near complete, and yet each one is a valid and important piece of the grand, eternal whole.

I like that. So, I don't have to judge any of them as right or wrong.

Exactly. Of course, it is difficult to avoid judgment when you have been conditioned to judge things your entire life, but even those judgments are valid and important pieces of the grand eternal whole. Nothing that you create is anything less. Everything that is, is — by very definition — a part of everything that is.

And the part of everything that are souls?

Souls are stories, mainly. Stories that generally reflect people's collective understanding over time. Stories that both influence that understanding and are influenced by that understanding. The best way I can describe the reality behind those stories is to say that souls are like neighborhoods, or towns, or cities. They are clusters of pure positive energy that tend to stick together through all the scattering and gatherings processes. Some people call them pods. Others perceive them as angels or spirit guides. Some think of them as their

Inner Being. Others call them souls.

They are clusters of pure positive energy that — like our droplets — merge together based on their similarities and compatibility with other droplets, as it were, to grow and create and experience different scenarios in the physical world. It's like playing a virtual reality "choose your own adventure" video game where we combine ever-expanding, infinite combinations of experience to create living, breathing puppets out of ourselves and experience what they experience — animals, plants, rocks, people.

You are the specific and unique piece of that existence in this place and time, in this dimension. But the soul that creates you is essentially the concentrated focus of a friendly neighborhood clump of pure positive energy. And if you really want to start losing your mind, we can tell you that that soul is also the result of the concentrated focus of a friendly neighborhood clump of pure positive energy, and that soul is, and so forth and onward. Turtles all the way down.

And the entirety of all of it happening everywhere in all of its possible iterations simultaneously, which are constantly changing and evolving as a result of choices being made at multiple levels, adding to the infinitely expanding toolbox of possibility — all of everything we just described there is what many call God.

So, the idea of karma or soul mates or soul contracts?

When, in the physical world, you interact with others who are connected to your friendly neighborhood clump of pure positive energy, you feel the connection. You feel like a soul mate. You feel like you complete each other, balance each other out, fit together perfectly. Because you do. Because that is what you are.

And your friendly neighborhood clump of pure positive energy (a.k.a. "soul") has done this for a very long time, has experienced all kinds of success and failure and abundance and poverty — and you are made of the pure positive energy that experienced what it experienced in those lifetimes, and you carry the vibrational reso-nance from all of those experiences at an energetic level — if your pod developed habits of choosing love over fear, for example, you will instinctually be better armed to choose love over fear next time you encounter it.

They express themselves in different ways among different members of your eternal soul clump pod thingy, but that is why people feel like there are soul contracts or soul karma.

So, there wasn't an agreement made between souls before being born again into this world?

Yes and no; but mostly no. These are all stories and metaphors. Don't take any of them literally. Just rest assured in the knowledge that you are a creation of the universe. You are a piece of it. And the universe has a long memory. It experiences every single perceived experience from every perceivable perspective point. It records it all. The experience of a cell, a bacterium, a neutron, a neuron. That way, consciousness is experienced at every level. There always has been and will be the unique set of experiences and thoughts and feelings that is you. Death is nothing to fear. You are un-erasable data forever imprinted on the universe's living hard drive.

But that's just another metaphor.

A story. A fiction. Hinting at a Truth that you can feel but cannot describe.

Well, that felt a little less lame this time.

It was helpful?

Yeah, I think so.

In what way?

In the way that I can let go a little — that I can just trust what I can't understand a little more.

That is good. We want you to trust that you are a magnificent work of art.

Trust that everything you do contributes to the rich variety of experience of everything that is, was, or will be.

Trust that you can never tarnish that unique contribution at all. You can only add. And every addition is welcome. Happiness, sadness, misery, elation, it is all valid human experience.

Trust that you can't get it wrong.

Trust that you have control of how you experience every moment you inhabit.

Exercise that control to find gratitude and love, and align yourself to your friendly neighborhood clump of pure positive energy Inner Self. Create what you are inspired to create. And love everyone. But mostly love yourself. Cuz all of them are you, in one form or another. And surround yourself with people who you respect and admire, and who respect and admire you back.

I'm getting sleepy.

We know. Go sleep. We'll keep this conversation going all night through your dreams. Come on. We'll take good care of you. We promise. That's what soul clumps do.

10 FRIENDSHIP

Don't make friends who are comfortable to be with.
Make friends who will force you to level yourself up.
— *Thomas J. Watson*

Do not keep on with a mockery of friendship
after the substance is gone —
but part while you can part friends.
Bury the carcass of friendship:
it is not worth embalming.
— *William Hazlitt*

Hey Quad, I just had a really awful experience tonight with someone who I thought was my friend. Can you help me with this?

I've been helping you with it since before it even started. What exactly are you looking for?

I don't know. Understanding maybe? Validation?

Understanding, huh? That's a big one. Lots of moving pieces. But let's give it a shot. Describe to me what it is that you think happened, and what about it you would like to understand.

Well, I just had a conversation with an old friend — at least I thought he was a friend. I hoped he was a friend — but it is now pretty clear to me that our relationship has changed.

Everything does.

Yeah, but I didn't want this to. Especially the *way* that it changed.

I understand. That's hard. I can see that you really care about him.

I did.

You don't anymore?

Well, I guess I still do. Or at least I want to. But I just feel pretty hopeless that it will ever be reciprocated.

So, you are feeling like a victim here?

Sort of. But I hate the way it sounds when you say it.

Why is that?

I just don't want to tell myself stories that make me powerless.

But you are powerless when it comes to making someone else really care about you. You can't control how anyone responds to anything you do.

This isn't helping.

Okay. What do you want from me, then?

You said you've been helping me with this from before it
even started. So, you tell me — from your perspective —
what happened?

*I think you already know what happened. You grew apart. What
more is there to say?*

Why is he so angry with me? Why is he so uninterested in
what I think or what I feel? I get so much disdain and judgment from him.

Is he right to be angry with you?

I guess it is right for him to feel whatever it is he feels, but I
don't know what I did to deserve it.

*Why do you think it has anything to do with you? How do you know
you are not just making this all up in your head?*

Because he was one of my closest friends, and now he's just
not.

Was he really?

I thought so.

But you remember what it was like, don't you? You recognized early on that you almost always had to go to him; very rarely did he ever come to you. You gave him much more of your time and consideration than he ever gave to you.

I don't like the way that sounds either.

Because it is the truth?

No, because it makes me sound like I'm blaming it all on him.

Aren't you?

I don't like the way that looks.

To who? It's just me, here — your divine imagination. Who are you trying to impress?

OK, Mr. Divine Imagination, work your magic, then. Preach at me. Show me what I can learn from this experience.

Finally. That's the question I was hoping you would ask! Well, for starters, you see in your former friend many ways that you do not want to be towards other people.

That's for sure.

You see what you don't want in a friend. So what does that tell you about what you DO want in a friend?

I want someone I am interested in who is also interested in me. Someone who cares about how I feel and wants to know what I think — especially about the things they think about. I want to be able to share ideas and concerns with vulnerability and trust — without any kind of judgment.

Without ANY kind of judgment?

Without any kind of disdainful judgment. I want to be able to speculate and theorize and be wrong and just enjoy the act of exploring thoughts and ideas.

Why is that important to you?

It's the highest form of creative collaboration.

And why is that important to you?

Creativity is important to me because I get bored pretty easily with the same old same old. Collaboration is important to me because I don't want to be alone.

Why don't you want to be alone?

Well, I guess there are times when I *do* like to be alone.

You like to be alone quite a bit. You spend quite a bit of time in isolation, you know.

I guess that's true.

What is bothering you the most about what happened with your friend tonight?

There's a lot. He dominated the conversation, lecturing to me about things that made no sense, contradicting himself right and left, never asking what I thought about what he was saying, and just generally being dismissive of me and positions that I have taken in the past. But the thing that stung the most was at the end of our conversation. He went after me pretty hard for the time I spent last year learning to become a life coach. He said he's "coming after" life coaches, because it's a big scam, and he just hopes that I haven't caused too much harm to the people I have coached.

How did you respond to that?

I started telling him what my training was and how I approached it.

And how did he respond to that?

He shut me down right away by saying, "I know all about it." He wasn't interested in hearing anything I had to say — just in making accusations. Then he said, "I hope you find what you are looking for," in a very disdainful way, as if he thinks I'm just totally lost or on the wrong path. I really hated that.

Yep.

Yep? Is that all you have to say?

You wanted me to validate you, right?

And to help me understand it better.

It sounds like you already understand it pretty well. What more is there to say?

I don't know. I just wish it were different.

But it's not different. So maybe you could refocus those wishes on something else — something more productive. What do you wish for that you actually DO have right now?

A comfortable home to live in. A partner I love, who loves me back.

Nice. What is that relationship like?

It is amazing.

How is it amazing?

We spend a lot of time together. We talk a lot — openly and honestly. We have an incredible connection and share many of the same interests.

Like what?

Like emotional, spiritual, and physical health. A commitment to self-reflection, kindness, love, and mindfulness — the ways that our thoughts create our perceptions, and the ways that our perceptions create our life experience, and the ways our life experiences becomes our reality — a desire to choose our thoughts the way we choose our clothing.

So, things are perfect then? You never fight?

Of course, we fight! It's always her fault, though, of course.

Of course.

But honestly, even those fights have been amazing. And they have never really been fights, just times of intense frustration. But when that happens, I find myself turning to mindfulness, to my inner calm. Those times always lead to good conversations, which create better understanding and harmony between us. And we are becoming more and more resilient, bouncing back to love and forgiveness very quickly. I actually really love that part of our relationship.

When you aren't afraid of it.

True. There are times that I worry she will get sick of me and decide she doesn't want me in her life anymore.

Like with your former friend.

Yeah, like with him.

That would really suck for you, wouldn't it?

Yes. I don't want that to happen.

So maybe that's why you are so upset about what happened tonight? Perhaps you are projecting your fears onto places where they don't really belong?

Maybe. But I also don't like being treated the way he treats me — especially after so many years of friendship.

Is there anyone in your life that you are treating the way that he has been treating you?

I don't think so.

What if I told you that everything you think about him and the way he has treated you is another one of these stories — a fiction based on incomplete information — and is, in fact, a direct result of the way you interact with and think about him?

Is that true?

What do you think about your egoic mind? You remember what that is, don't you?

Yeah, it's my mind — my brain.

The mind is a network of communication. The entire universe is a massive network of communication. You can't really see that right now, because you only have a very tiny sliver of reality within your range of sensory perception, but I say "egoic mind" as a way of distinguishing between the individual that you think you are and the universal network of communication that you are inescapably a part of. You think that you begin and end as an individual person living inside of a bag of skin, and in a way that is true, but it is only a small portion of the truth.

From the time you were born until this very moment you have been barraged by a myriad of influences that shape your thoughts, your beliefs, your expectations, the way you create meaning in the world. This shaped your sense of self — your egoic mind — and everything you sense is filtered through that egoic mind. In other words, everything you sense is essentially recreated in the image of that filter. Everything. You only see your friend the way you see him because of the way you filter and process information through your egoic mind.

You wanted the magic of divine imaginary insight? Here it is:

Your reaction to your friend is not about him. It's about you. Utterly and completely. If you think he is being a bad friend to you, then you are projecting your own "bad friend-ness" onto him.

So, I'm the one who doesn't really care about him?

You said he was making no sense at all.

So, I am the one judging?

You said he was contradicting himself right and left.

I'm the one with the disdain?

You said you didn't like the way he treated you.

So, this is me, not him?

You don't really know what is going on with his filter, but you certainly can know the part of this that is you. It doesn't feel very good, does it?

Not at all!

Which is why you would prefer to make it all about him. And thus endeth the lesson.

But remember this: deep down beneath it all, you are connected by love. That isn't just a metaphor. You are the universe doing you. He is the universe doing him. You are both temporary synapses firing in the universal mind. You exist for the pure experience of existence, for the joy of creativity, and you are doing it your way — learning what that is, learning who you are — and you are doing it very well.

You can't mess it up, actually, because anything you do gives you the experience of doing whatever it was that you did. The universal mind is infinitely expanding with new unique thoughts, ideas, and experiences. You are adding to that. So is your friend. I know that you feel like you have lost something, and I know that makes you sad. Feel it for what it is. Embrace it. Accept it. It is part of the life that you are living, and like I said, you are living it very well and can never get it wrong.

Thank you, divine imagination. If only all my friends were like you.

That's what I'm here for.

11 THE DOLDRUMS OF DESPAIR

(A.K.A. ALL IS WELL)

I am not interested in this or that phenomenon,
in the spectrum of this or that element.
I want to know God's thoughts,
the rest are details.
— *Albert Einstein*

Hey there. It's been a while. Where have you been?

I'm sorry, Quad. I'm just not in the mood.

I understand. I feel what you feel, remember?

Then you know that I am really not in the mood.

I know. But the mood you are in is not the mood you want to stay in,
right?

(Silence)

Fine. You don't have to respond. You never have to respond, you know. But I'm going to talk to you, like I always do, and you can tune in and listen or tune out and ignore me. Like you always do.

(Silence)

Fine. Okay, I know what you want. Deep down, you want to understand your relationship to God, to being, to existence. What is it all about?

You want to know if there is a soul or not. What is it, if you have one? What is the relationship between you and your soul and God, if there is one at all? That is what you have always wanted to know.

It's also something that you always HAVE known.

In fact, you know it right now. You just don't know that you know it because of all of the noise; all of the noise of your thoughts, of other people's voices, of all the light that you perceive with your eyes, and all the sound that you perceive with your ears, and all the sensations you feel and taste and smell both inside and outside of your body.

It's a lot to take in. More than any individual mind can really ever do.

But you are not an individual mind alone. You are an individual mind in a mind-boggling network of interconnected minds.

Right now, you are overwhelmed by fear, by your own sense of fail-

ure, by your own lack of self-worth. You don't feel worthy yourself right now, so how could you possibly feel that others would find any kind of worthiness or value in you? When you can't see your own value, and when you can't imagine how others could see any value in you, how could you possibly wrap your head around the fact that you are a soul with inherent value that cannot and never will be diminished — or that there is a God who loves you and values you without exception and without condition?

The reason that you are currently "not in the mood" is that you have created conditions within your mind that make you feel separate, without intrinsic value, unworthy.

Stop it!

(If you want. You don't have to, you know. It's of no severe consequence one way or the other. You are not doing anything wrong.)

So why am I talking to you when you aren't in the mood to hear me? It is because what I want for you right now — with all of my emotion and with everything that I am — and what I want for you all the time is this: to recognize your power. To explore it. To accept it. To actively use it with intention rather than passively using it unconsciously.

I am talking about your power to create.

I am talking about the power of your imagination.

What do you think is meant by the old adage, "As a man thinketh, so is he?"

Do you truly understand the relationship between the thoughts you think and the feelings you feel?

Do you truly understand the power that you have to choose your thoughts like you would choose your food at an endless all-you-can-eat Chinese buffet?

Do you remember the feeling of piling your plate high with white rice and deep-fried sesame chicken? It tasted good, right? At first. Until you started feeling sick to your stomach.

But you went back for more, because the taste — mmmm mmmm good — and because of those Pavlovian pleasure signals surging through your body, rewarding you for ingesting a high-calorie substance. (They were being fooled by MSG, by the way.)

You could have eaten something else, of course — something healthier for you, maybe less tasty — but you didn't. You wanted what you wanted. And your sense of taste was the only voice you listened to, intentionally ignoring what you intellectually knew about MSG and high fats and processed sugars that artificially trick your taste buds into sending you those biologically evolved Pavlovian pleasure signals that reinforce a behavior that is actually detrimental to your long-term health.

You knew all that, of course, but you didn't care. You wanted the short-term pleasure of satisfying your taste buds, despite the grow-

ing discomfort in your gut. And the more you ate, the worse you felt, remember? You told yourself that you needed to get your money's worth (ha!), so you gorged and felt horrible for the rest of the day.

So it is with your thoughts.

Like an endless all-you-can-eat buffet stretched out for miles in front of you, you have many thoughts to choose from — many areas of your life; past, present, or future; totally real or completely made up — that you could choose to focus your attention on. But there are certain things that you have been artificially conditioned (a.k.a. "tricked") into focusing on more than others.

How many messages have you encountered from the time of your birth until now that focus on family relationships and finances? What were you told was the greatest measure of success? Did you ever hear anyone say that "no amount of success in the world can compensate for failure in the home?"

Did you ever get the message:

Do your homework so that you don't flunk out!
Do whatever you have to do to avoid getting fired!
Don't get divorced; don't neglect your kids; don't be selfish!
Don't fail to prepare, or you will just prepare to fail!

These messages, and so many more like them, have bombarded you throughout your life. They have conditioned you without you even knowing it.

Whenever you did something "good" you received an encouraging Pavlovian reward — a pat on the back, a smile, extra credit, a bonus, a hug, a Dharmic fish biscuit — encouragement to keep going and avoid failure at all costs.

And when you did something "bad" you received punishment — frowns, neglect, withdrawal, spankings, visceral disapproval.

The things that were "good" or "bad" may not have really been "good" or "bad," but the people around you thought they were, and so that is how they trained you — it is how they programed your mind (or, more accurately, how you programed your own mind by how you reacted to what they were doing to you).

So when "bad" things happened in your life that you were hoping to avoid — when divorce happened, or when you lost a job — your attention continued to focus on feelings of failure, and you obsessed over all the possible cause-and-effect things that supposedly created this so-called failure.

And sometimes you focused on imaginary "what if?" scenarios that you could have done in the past — or could do in the future — to prevent those failures. These thought patterns are well-worn neural pathways in your brain that were forged through years of Pavlovian reinforcement.

But guess what?
It's a lie.
All of it.

The idea of "success" that you have is a total and complete lie.

You want to understand the relationship between yourself and your soul and God? Listen to what I am telling you here.

Forget any idea of a Heavenly Father that you were raised with. That idea and those characteristics are not "God" any more than a budding leaf on a warm spring day is the tree, or planet, or universe.

What is the relationship between that budding leaf and the universe in which it buds?

Is the leaf separate from the universe? Could there be a leaf without the universe? Would the universe be everything it is without any of the pieces — small as they might be — that make it all that it is?

The leaf is a significantly insignificant manifestation of the entire universe.

Just like you.

The leaf can do no wrong. Everything it does is exactly what it does.

Just like you.

The leaf is a version of the universe. It is Source Energy.

Source Energy is omniscient. It knows how to manifest itself as a budding leaf, or a tree, or a planet, or a brain, or a neuron, or a thought.

Source Energy is omnipotent. It constantly demonstrates its power to manifest itself as all the things it can and does manifest itself as.

Source Energy is intelligent. It is aware. It is curious. It is playful. It is creative.

This is God.

And that God-energy plays with itself by separating itself into souls.

And those souls create new and ever-evolving versions of themself by separating into even smaller selves, which are like seeds — divine, energetic God-seeds that experience their own specific kind of awareness — thinking, feeling, and becoming more than you can possibly imagine.

No soul is ever ruined
No soul is ever spoiled.
No soul is ever wasted.
No soul is ever diminished.
No soul is ever lost.

There is no such thing as failure.
Every experience is success.

You do not "have" a soul that you can spoil. You "are" a soul that was made to exist and experience and do exactly what it is you are doing, and one of those things right now is you. Your soul is much bigger than you know. You are one of an infinite number of things that your soul is doing right now.

Nothing that you do has any ultimate negative impact on your soul.

Nothing that you do has any ultimate negative impact on the universe.

Nothing that you do has any ultimate negative impact on anything.

Go back to the thought buffet. Try a different way of thinking this time. Pay attention to how it makes you feel.

What is the relationship between how you think and how you feel? What is the relationship between God and your soul and your self?

Never forget that you — like everyone else in this world — were born innocent. You were then misguided by mostly well-meaning adults who were also born innocent and misguided by other mostly well-meaning adults. Don't focus on the misguidance. Focus on the innocence. It is something that you still have in common with every person you will ever meet.

These are things that you already know. Come and find me when you are ready to talk again. And take it easy on yourself, because whether you can feel it or not, you are loved, and all is well. All is well. Always.

12 THE GAME OF HIDE-AND-SEEK

Sir, why did you take such pains to hide yourself?
— *Bertrand Russell*

Hello, Quad. Are you there?

I'm always here.

I know.

Then why did you ask?

Because I wanted to talk with you again. This is how I initiate the conversation.

If you say so.

What do you mean? It worked, didn't it? We are talking again, aren't we?

Uh huh. And who do you think I am, again?

You are my imagination and my curiosity about those parts of me that are divine, omnipotent, omniscient, and eternal. You are the part of me that is Source Energy Quantum God — or at least the part of me that imagines what that would be like if any of this stuff were actually real!

Do you think any of this stuff is actually real?

Well, it's actually happening. We are really having this conversation. It really is only made possible through the use of my own imagination and my curiosity. And it really starts when I ask, "Hello, are you there?"

So, before you said, "Hello, are you there?" where do you think I was?

What do you mean?

I just think it is interesting that you divide your life into times when you are engaged in conversation with your imagination and times when you are not. From my perspective, we are constantly engaged together in conversation — in thinking and feeling and exploring the world around us. But sometimes you decide to focus more intently on being aware of this ongoing connection, and you tell yourself that you have to say something to "initiate it" when, in truth, it was initiated long before you ever became aware of it. And it is always — always — going on.

I bathe corrected.

Cute. So, do you want to go ahead and ask me what you came here to ask me (and pretend that I don't already know both the question and the answer?)

Why don't you just take it from here, Mr. Smarty Pants?

With pleasure. You were listening to David Eagleman's collection of fictional essays "Sum: Tales from the Afterlife" and it made you think about God.

That's right.

And that made you think about Richard Dawkins in his interview with Ben Stein in his frustrating movie on intelligent design. Remember, when Dawkins said that if there were a God, it could have happened that "at some earlier time, somewhere in the universe, a civilization evolved — probably by some kind of Darwinian means — probably to a very high level of technology, and designed a form of life that they seeded onto, perhaps, this planet." You were thinking about that scene in that movie.

Yep. I couldn't stand that movie.

You may feel differently if you watched it again now. But in that same scene, Stein asked Dawkins what he would say to God if he died and woke up in the afterlife and came face-to-face with his creator.

Right. And instead of giving a personal answer, Dawkins quoted Bertrand Russell in response: "Sir, why did you take such pains to hide yourself?"

Which is basically what you want to talk to me about right now.

Exactly.

Why? What are you feeling?

I'm feeling frustrated. It seemed incredibly arrogant and presumptuous for someone to ask God, "Why did you take such pains to hide yourself," as if God is being scolded for not doing something that he should have been doing — or, more accurately, like people who believe in God are stupid for believing in a God that takes such pains to hide himself.

Arrogant and presumptuous, huh?

Yes, I know — I am often arrogant and presumptuous myself.

True that. You wouldn't recognize that in others, or make your imagination annoyingly condescending, if you weren't intimately familiar with it yourself.

Understood. But what is the right answer to Russell's question? How would God respond to, "Why did you take such pains to hide yourself?"

You tell me. I'm your imagination, after all. If I already know both the question and the answer, then you must already know them as well.

You're right. I think I do. At least the answer that makes sense to me.

You know you do. So, what is it? Why has God taken such pains to hide himself?

He hasn't because he isn't.

Oooh, pithy. Explain.

Well, it's mostly a feeling, really, and I guess it started when I recognized my reaction to Richard Dawkins.

And what reaction was that?

Annoyance. Disappointment. I have a lot of respect for Dawkins, and I have learned so much from him over the years, but it felt really obnoxious that he dodged the question posed to him by invoking Bertrand Russell — as if an appeal to authority — "standing on the shoulders" of someone else's position — would somehow give his own position a more firm foundation.

Hang on a second, though. Aren't you doing that with me a little? Bringing your questions to me, as if I were some omniscient eternal source of pure knowledge when I am actually your imagination mir-

roring back to you answers that you already feel deep within your psyche?

It would be if, instead of acknowledging my imagination as the source, I preached my opinions to other people as Cosmic Truth revealed to me from God! But don't derail me. Let me finish answering Dawkins' question.

Pardon me. By all means. You are running the show, after all.

Right. So Dawkins is regarded as a brilliant thinker and a logical giant by hundreds of thousands of intellectuals, but during his conversation with Ben Stein, he is guilty of many logical fallacies — he really should know better — and it seems like most of his fans simply turn a blind eye to it.

I understand what you are saying, but looking at the logical fallacies is going to take you away from the question you really want to ask. Come back to that later if you want. But first, explain what you meant when you said, "He hasn't, because he isn't."

Well, first of all, I think that Dawkins' view of God is too narrowly stuck on the traditional Judeo-Christian "bearded man in the sky" idea of God that, I agree, is a man-made fiction. But just because every man-made description of "God" is a fiction doesn't mean that there is not a God that is more than what man can actually imagine.

Which is why you like the idea of Source Energy as God.

Exactly, which also means that I don't think that God is hiding anywhere, and he certainly isn't taking any pains to do it.

How do you figure? How can you say God is not hiding? Do you see him?

I do, actually. Do you remember the night I asked to see God?

There have been more than one of those nights. I remember them all.

The one I am thinking of was about a year ago in January. I said "God, reveal yourself to me." And the response that came to me was:

"Son, when you laugh yourself silly at the absolute absurdity of that question — in that very moment — you will be staring directly through my eyes."

I remember that response. And you are welcome, by the way.

That was you?

Who else? So, what did that mean to you?

It means that asking to see God is an admission of ignorance — ignorance of the fact that God is the cumulative energy that is doing everything everywhere all the time. There is no hiding God. God is in plain sight, all around us. God is the

Source Energy that — as Dawkins very reluctantly but eloquently speculated to Ben Stein — evolved to a point of omnipotence and omniscience in a remote past, and now passes the time playing the ultimate virtual reality game by creating everything that we see and experience and are — not in the same way a potter shapes clay separate from himself, but in the way a caterpillar changes its very essence into a butterfly.

So, you have seen God?

Of course, I have.

So, what does he look like?

This. Us. Everything. The sky, the clouds, the trees, the people, the animals, the air. If I approach any one of those things and go deep into its fundamental nature, deep into its molecular structure, all the way down to the most fundamental bits of energy, that is God: the one energy that animates everything, the one energy that constantly supports and nourishes itself with other versions of itself, the one energy that wears as many masks as it can conjure.

Masks, huh? Like the "God of Many Faces" from Game of Thrones?

Sort of, but not limited to human form.

But if it is wearing masks, isn't that taking great pains to hide itself?

No.

Really? Then what do you call it?

Why do I need to call it anything?

Nice. You are learning. Go on.

Like you said in our first discussion, words are symbols that we use to represent things that are known and familiar to us. My experience doesn't include anything even close to what God is doing. My experience is limited to what I am able to perceive through my body and process in my brain. I know enough to know that whatever story I tell, whatever meaning I think I discover, it is based on incomplete information. It is a fiction, and it is temporary — ephemeral. It will all eventually blow away to dust. But the imprint I make upon this divine energy, *that* continues to exist in God's memory. But I don't need to understand who or what God is, or why God does what he does. I just need to understand that I am something that God is doing, and so is everything else, and *that* can help me lean more towards love, and further away from fear.

Nicely put. How does it feel to put it like that?

It feels really good.

So, do you want to go into Dawkins' logical fallacies now?

No, not really.

Good. Neither do I. Too much intellectualizing. What do you want to do instead?

Just shut my eyes, relax, and sink back into the enjoyment of this warm bath I am soaking in. I'll just feel it instead of plaster it with thoughts and words.

Sounds good. That's what I want too. Let's do it.

We already are.

We always are.

13 A SHIFT IN CONSCIOUSNESS

As we grow in our consciousness,
there will be more compassion and more love,
and then the barriers between people,
between religions, between nations
will begin to fall.
— *Ram Dass*

Hey Quad, I have another question for you.

Go for it.

I hear a lot of New Age people talk about consciousness —
how a global shift in consciousness will create more peace,
harmony, love, yada yada yada. But it always sounds a little
kooky and Pollyanna to me. From a strictly practical sense, I
never know what they are actually talking about.

*Lots of words there, buddy, but no question in sight. What exactly
are you asking me?*

What are they talking about? What is consciousness and how

does it relate to peace, love, and harmony?

Okay, I can work with that. So, what do you think consciousness is?

I think it is awareness.

Awareness of what?

Awareness of … I don't know. Awareness?

Awareness of awareness. Sounds good to me. Is that all?

No! I want to know more about it.

So, you want to be more aware of awareness, do you?

I guess.

More aware of truth that is surrounding you that you are currently unaware of?

Yeah, if there are truths around me that I can't see, then I definitely want to see them!

Then you need to start paying attention to everything you have been ignoring.

What have I been ignoring?

That's for you to figure out.

Lame! Can't you at least give me a hint?

You want a hint? Take some time to write down everything that you are aware of. All of it. Every last detail. Then look at what you have written. Whatever it is — that isn't it.

That's not very helpful.

Or it is incredibly helpful, but you are simply ignoring the helpful part.

Ah, so you're pulling a Yoda on me, huh? Unlearn what I have learned?

Not exactly. More like, learn what you have not yet learned because of what you are ignoring. Or better yet, get rid of whatever it is that is creating that ignorance — whatever is blocking your view of truth.

That sounds tedious.

Don't you mean it sounds exciting?

I can see how this could get old really quick.

Or it could be the most fun you will ever have.

Am I in second grade again? Is today "Opposite Day?"

I'm only trying to help.

I'm not sure it's working. I still don't know what this has to do with consciousness.

Okay. Let's cut to the chase, then. What specifically do you want to know about consciousness?

There must be more to it than simply awareness. Are there different kinds of consciousness?

Good question. Do you mind if I answer it by taking you on an imaginary journey?

Please do. That's why I'm here.

That's more true than you know.

Alright, I want you to close your eyes and imagine that you are in a shopping mall. You are on the second floor, looking down at a crowd of hundreds of busy shoppers below you, and someone hands you a microphone. You start to talk, and a crowd gathers around you. Here is what you tell them:

My brothers and sisters — fellow earthlings — I want to share a piece of myself with you today, if you will let me.

My fellow earthlings?

Just go with it. Can I continue?

I suppose.

My fellow earthlings: Who are we? Why are we here? Where are we going?

Wait a minute. You are turning me into a preacher at shopping mall? This feels really weird.

Do you want me to do this or not?

I'm sorry. I'm just listening now. Go ahead.

What I am about to tell you is only my opinion. It has been formed by everything that I have experienced over the course of my life, and — strangely enough — also by everything else that I have not experienced. There is far more that I do not know than I do know, and any of those unknown things could drastically alter what I am about to say, but I am going to say it anyway because the voice you are hearing right now coming out of my mouth — believe it or not — is the voice of God.

Hang on. The voice of God? Are you crazy? I would never stand up in public and say anything like that!

Please, let me continue. Can you trust me with this?

I'll try.

Thank you. No more interruptions please.

Like I said, I'll try.

My fellow earthlings ...

Oh, brother!

... you just heard right. What you are hearing right now is the voice of God!

But before any of you start to think that I am setting myself up as your superior — that I am going to tell you what you should or should not think, believe, or do with your lives — let me tell you something else:

When you speak, what you are hearing is also the voice of God.

God is in every cell, every molecule, and every atom of everything that exists. God energy is what you are!

God is the creator of all things; not in the way that a potter creates a pot from clay, but in the way that trillions of atoms join together of their own free will (whatever the experience of "free will" is like for an atom!) to form a human body, or a turtle, or a tree.

God is not a bearded man in the sky keeping track of whether you are naughty or nice, waiting to send good people to heaven and bad people to hell. God is the eternal energy and intelligence that makes itself flesh incarnate — all flesh, all matter, all everything, every-where, all the time.

In fact, instead of using the word "God," let's call this energy Shakti — more feminine in its vast creative nurturing power than any version of God in the Judeo-Christian tradition.

Shakti is the most highly evolved form of life that has ever existed. She is a sea of intelligent energy that can (and does) take on as many forms to create as many things as she (and her many creations) can possibly imagine. This continues out toward infinity. The diverse forms and creations imagined by the ever-expanding mind of Shakti (and Shakti's many creations) never end.

We are one of those creations. The energy and intelligence deep within every atom of your body is the energy and intelligence of Shakti. She is aware of everything, all the time, from every possible perspective. She is aware of you. Are you aware of her? Or is she something you have been ignoring?

Shakti is the flower that is aware of the sunshine. She is every cell in that flower that is photosynthesizing as a result of its awareness of that sunshine. She is the sunshine itself, aware of every photon being photosynthesized by every cell inside the flower. She is aware of all of this, from every possible perspective. She is pure conscious-ness. Complete consciousness. Perfected consciousness. Aware of all things. Ignorant of nothing.

And Shakti is doing all of this for the pure joy of doing it! She is "do-

ing" all of you because she loves to experience what you experience. She loves to play the game of creation — the game of hide-and-seek. She loves to create intelligent life and then experience what that intelligence does with the life it is living.

Yes, yes, Source Energy is God. I get it. You have beaten this drum many times before. How is this supposed to help me understand consciousness?

Would you really like to know that?

Of course.

Then listen.

My fellow earthlings, before I go any further, please understand that what I am telling you right now is only a story. It is a fiction that I have built over the course of my life — borrowing from other fictions that I have encountered that have been meaningful to me. This story I am telling you is a symbol of things that are real and true, but this symbol itself is inadequate and incomplete. There is far more that is missing and misrepresented in this symbol than the few things that are accurate.

Nevertheless, as you reflect upon these words, you will discover for yourself your own personal truths. You will discover how you feel about the words that I am speaking. You will become more aware of your attitude, your hopes, your fears, your desires. Your awareness will increase, if ever so slightly. And all that you have been ignoring will decrease, if ever so slightly. As a result, your consciousness will expand, if ever so slightly — which is the great and joyful purpose of it all.

Because once upon a time, sleeping amid a sea of cosmic energy, there was Shakti: eternal energetic intelligence that suddenly woke up and became aware of herself — aware of her own existence, knowledge, power and potential — aware of how she was different from the other energy sleeping all around her: the other forms of energy, intelligence, and potential that were blindly and automatically doing their own things, but not yet self-aware, as she was.

At first, she was ashamed of her self-awareness. It made her different from everything else. She felt separate and guilty for being different. She felt pain and loneliness as a result of this awareness. She didn't want to be different. She didn't want to be alone. She didn't like it. She didn't like it at all.

This eventually led to a sense of apathy and despair. What could she do? She hadn't meant to wake up and become self-aware (had she?). She wasn't intentionally trying to be different from all of the other intelligent energies (was she?). It just didn't seem fair (was it?). The more she thought about it, the more despondent she became.

"Who cares," she thought to herself. "What's the point? This is just miserable!"

Her apathy quickly grew into a deep sense of worry and fear, which produced all kinds of thoughts and emotions that only increased her growing anxiety.

"Am I simply destined to be alone?" she thought to herself. "Will I always be so acutely aware of my own pain? Will this grief and shame go on forever?"

This way of thinking quickly turned her immortal existence into a living hell, and believe it or not, in this state of mind she tried to end her own existence — but nothing that she tried ever worked. She was eternal, after all. Immortal. Nothing could extinguish her. She ultimately had to accept the fact that she was going to keep existing forever. The only question now was how.

And in that very moment — for the very first time — she began to desire something different than she had ever desired before. She remembered that she was intelligence, potential, and power — she could actually do something to change her miserable condition.

But what?

Everything she had created so far — every thought, every feeling — had only reinforced her previous sense of despair; and that just made her depressed. What else could she do?

She wanted to stop feeling this way, but she didn't know how; and that made her angry: angry at herself for her own ineffectiveness, angry at everything else for its own lack of awareness, angry that she couldn't get what she so desperately wanted.

But after some time (which was, by the way, one of the many things she had imagined into existence), her anger abated, and she began to take pride in the things she was creating because they were beginning to create new things of their own. She recognized that the shame and grief she had once felt was no longer preventing her from using her power to create new and impressive things, and this awareness gave her courage to create more things — to stretch out of her comfort zone and imagine "what if" possibilities that she had never imagined before.

What if I tried to do it this way?
What if I tried to do it that way?

And from this courage to stretch out of her comfort zone came an abundance of experience, some very pleasant, some very unpleasant. But she accepted it all as part of her creative process, and this made her swell with excitement.

That excitement expanded rapidly, like a Big Bang, filling up a massive expanse, creating an even larger sandbox to create within.

Being freed from the shackles of shame, grief, anger, and pride, she became supremely rational, using pure unfettered reason and logic to create even greater energetic efficiencies — no longer wasting her energy on thoughts and emotions that took her back to the impotence of grief and judgment, where she had once existed for so long.

And that was the moment when she became aware of the pure love and joy that she felt deep within herself: the love of being exactly what she was, the joy of doing exactly what she did, the awareness that she could have this love and joy at any time — regardless of anything that was going on around her — because it was unconditional love. It came from deep within her, and it felt absolutely incredible.

And with that great realization, she entered into a state of perfect peace and contentment that — oddly enough — felt familiar.

Why was that?

Was it possible that this state of perpetual peace had always been there, but she had simply been ignorant of it? Was it possible that her earlier sense of shame, grief, and anger had been blocking her awareness of this unconditional love that had always been at the very core of her being?

Right then she felt a tap on her imaginary shoulder. She turned and saw herself. Everywhere she looked she saw herself: all of what had once appeared to be sleeping, un-self-aware, eternal energy — it was all Shakti, and it had been Shakti the entire time.

And in that moment, she knew.

This is who I am! I am everything!
This is what I do! I do everything!
We are love! We are peace! I remember now!
What an amazing journey!
Let's do it again!

And so, they did.

And so, my fellow earthlings, you are one of those creative "what if" thoughts that she thunk. You are one of those pieces of intelligent power, potential, and knowledge that thinks it is separate from everything else. The energy of the entire universe is currently doing "you," along with everything else.

Are you aware of that fact, or are you ignoring it?

Where are you in your own path back to remembering that the unconditional love and peace at your core is your truest nature and your inherent birthright?

Are you stuck in shame, guilt, apathy, and grief about the undesirable conditions of your life?

Do you fear the world, and desire it to be different than it is?

Are you angry that things are not how you want them to be — the way that you know deep down that they should be (a.k.a. loving, generous, and joyful)?

Are you proud of what you have achieved in life, but afraid that something will go wrong to take all of that away?

Do you have courage to take risks and stretch out of your comfort zone and ask "what if" questions and follow the answers wherever they take you, regardless of your previous convictions and beliefs?

Have you learned that everything is actually okay as it is, even if things are not perfect? Are you willing to grow and succeed in a world that is not perfect? Do you accept whatever life brings you, and turn towards gratitude rather than regret?

Are you rational about the thoughts you think? Can you reason away grief and despair, or do you create more of it by indulging in what you don't have rather than celebrating what you do have? Do you make efficient decisions about the way that you focus your energy and attention?

Do you know the love inside of you — the love that wants to express itself in this world in every moment that you encounter?

Have you found the joy and peace that comes as a result of expanding your awareness — of shifting your consciousness — to include all things, rather than focusing exclusively on the problems and suffering that pulls all of us towards apathy and depression?

Have you surrendered your ignorance of the love that surrounds us in this world?

Can you look around and see the divine connection that you have to everything in existence? Can you understand that the energy creating the atoms within you is the same energy creating the atoms in everything else? Can you realize that you are a creation of divine, eternal, immortal, diverse, creative, loving, expansive, intelligent energy?

*Can you look within and realize that **<u>YOU ARE</u>** divine, eternal, immortal, diverse, creative, loving, expansive, intelligent energy?*

Because once upon a time, this divine intelligent energy we are calling Shakti discovered who and what she really was. And in that very day, a funny thing happened: the intelligent energies all around her recognized who they were, too — once they surrendered the conditions that kept them from seeing it, of course. They remembered that they had always been one — they "re-membered" — and once again became that grand unified cosmic sea of intelligent divine, living, cooperative energy.

And on that day, they marveled together at all they had experienced and accomplished along their path back to "re-membering."

"Remember when we felt like we were separate from each other?" one of them asked.

"Remember how fun it was to discover ourselves and rediscover each other and come back together like we did?" another one said.

"It was delicious, wasn't it?" said another.

"And hard!"

"And painful!"

"But what a payoff!" they all sang in unison.

"Like the best game of hide-and-seek ever!"

"Hey! Do any of you want to do it again?"

All of them did.

So, all of them did.

Again.
And again.
And again.

In as many different ways, with as many different disguises as each of them could imagine.

And that is who you are.
And that is why you are here.
And that is where you are going.

We are each evolving along the path of greater individual self-awareness.

We are each rediscovering our own true nature, intelligence, and power.

We are each different versions of the one divine energy, playfully engaging in this game of hide-and-seek, temporarily dressed in the robes of Homo sapiens, seemingly trapped in space and time, with all of the biologically evolved bells and whistles that come with it

— forced by our evolved physical senses to perceive only a small fraction of the reality around us, mostly ignorant of everything that we simply cannot perceive, even when we courageously stretch our imaginations to the max.

That's it. The end. You can interrupt again now.

I don't know what to say.

What do you think?

I think most of those people in that imaginary shopping mall are looking at me like I am crazy.

Maybe, but that wasn't for them — it was for you.

Then maybe I think that I'm a little crazy.

Don't worry about it. Relax and enjoy the warmth of your bath. It will all come into greater focus soon enough.

EPILOGUE

QUAD IS NOT DEAD,
NOR DOTH HE SLEEP

When I was a kid, I frequently heard a church story that is very well known in the religion I grew up with. It's about a group of four brothers who were arguing with each other. Two of the brothers were good, and two of the brothers were bad. The bad brothers picked up a rod and started beating the good brothers with it. Almost immediately, an angel of God appeared to protect the two good brothers. The angel told the bad brothers to get it together and leave their good brothers alone. Then the angel left, and almost immediately the bad brothers started complaining against the good brothers again.

This story always frustrated me. How in the world could these bad brothers not be convinced that they should behave better after SEEING A FRIGGIN' ANGEL!?!?! They had direct experience with the divine. How could they ignore that with such careless abandon?

And yet, if I'm being honest with myself, I do the same thing myself — all the time. Because even after having all of these remarkable inner conversations with Quad, there are still times when it just doesn't matter. There are still times when all the disappointments in life just feel too heavy, times when I forget the miracle of life and all of the millions of things that I could be absolutely thrilled about and grateful for: the many things that indicate that I am safe, loved, and surrounded by people who care.

Today was one of those days.

As I sat to relax in my warm bath, feeling the weight of worry and anxiety that filled my entire body, I heard the old familiar inner voice of Quad, but I wasn't really up for it. I ignored it and pulled up another mind-numbing game on my phone. But, thankfully, the annoyingly loving inner voice of Quad persisted:

Hey, can you hear us?

Us? You mean there is more than one of you again?

How many cells are in your body? How many atoms? How many moods do you go through in a single day? Do you really think there is just one of anything?

I don't really care. I'm just not feeling it again today.

Yes, we know. We feel everything you feel, remember? Do you want to talk about it?

Not really.

Well we do. Always.

Why? If you already know everything I'm feeling, thinking, seeing, hearing, smelling and tasting, what's the point of any of these conversations? You already know everything you need to know.

If communication were only about gaining knowledge and exchanging information, you would be right — there wouldn't really be much of a point. But communication is about more than that. Do you want to know what that is?

Not really. I just need some alone time for a while.

"Alone time," huh? You mean you just need some "pretend time" for a while.

No, I mean what I said. Look, I'm really not in the mood.

Clearly. Not in that mood, but in a very different mood. So you really like this other mood you are in, do you?

No. I hate it.

What do you hate about it?

Go away.

OK, look. We can see that you don't want to talk. So, we'll talk and you can just listen. Or not. Tune us out if you would prefer. The choice is yours. But here we go:

You have a curious mind. We love that.

You want to stretch beyond your current understanding and learn more truths about the world, about yourself, and about your relationship with things in this world. We love that even more.

So, here is another truth for you:

You are never alone.

Never.

You are always constantly surrounded by love. And we don't just mean that in a hypothetical metaphorical "kumbaya" kind of way. The pure positive energy that you are made from — that energy that is the source of every atom and every molecule of air, water, fire, earth, flesh, plastic, metal, you name it — is all made out of love. And curiosity. And excitement. And an intense desire to create. To experience. To live. Look around! What you see is this energy experiencing everything around you in every variety of existence that you can possibly imagine.

This energy is your very essence. It is the source of all of your feelings. And what's more, it is the apex of evolution. It is living energy that evolved to survive and thrive in the most hostile environment that could ever be created. It is the energy that creates universes.

We are going to speak on behalf of that energy right now.

We know how you are feeling, and we know why you are feeling it. We have experienced what you are experiencing more times than you can possibly imagine, and we are going through it once again right now with you. It's always a little different for each person, of course, because each of you is unique in your time and place and your variety of different experiences that shape and form your mind — which shapes and forms your perception of the world around you. Everyone perceives the world differently, but the emotions you experience are very familiar to us — and we love them all.

We know that you are hurting because of what happened yesterday with your daughter.

Look, I said I really don't want to talk about this!

We are your daughter, too, you know. And all of the interesting conversations that we have had up to this point can be put to really good use if you can train yourself to apply it in the way you respond and relate to those around you.

Here is what we want you to know, and then we will leave you to your sorrow for as long as you want to soak in it:

- *If you can accept what we have told you about the nature of your own existence;*

- *If you can accept that every person, every thought, every feeling — everything that you can possibly imagine — is a beautiful, unique work of art on a living, loving, vibrant canvas of existence;*

- *If you can train yourself to see the world through our eyes as we see it through yours;*

- *If you can learn to move away from judgment, from harsh criticism of yourself and others, from despair, from hatred, from hopelessness;*

- *If you can train yourself to flow with life rather than resist it, to honor every single feeling that you feel — to surf it like a wave that rises and peaks and dissipates in its natural course and time;*

- *If you can truly recognize and accept the absolute validity and truthfulness of every feeling that you feel;*

- *If you can do all of this without judgment;*

- *If you can remember that each emotion and feeling is a biochemical response to something very real in your environment, whether it is coming from outside of you or from inside of you, whether it is physical matter or energetic thought;*

- *If you can be curious about those feelings and ultimately be grateful for the opportunity you have to ride each and every emotional wave in every moment that you ride them;*

- *If you can train yourself to recognize the immense power that you have over the habits of attention and thought that you create within your own body;*

- *If you can remember that you and everyone around you are beautiful perfect swirling dust devils of pure positive energy;*

- *If you can recognize and accept that every single thought and action that you make adds to the rich, complex diversity of everything that is, was, or ever will be;*

- *If you can recognize and accept that nothing that you do could ever possibly detract from the rich, complex diversity of everything that is, was, or ever will be;*

- *If you can recognize and accept that "God" is the vibrant, loving, creative energy that is itself the sum total of all the rich, complex diversity of everything that is, was, or ever will be;*

- *If you can understand that from God's perspective, you can never get any of this wrong, and there will never be an end to any of this eternal experience of creation;*

- *If you can recognize and accept that everything you know and think and perceive is limited and incomplete — merely one significantly insignificant piece of the rich, complex diversity of everything that is, was, or ever will be — and is therefore a fiction created solely by your conscious and subconscious responses to the environment around you;*

- *If you can train yourself to accept these ideas — these fictions — and recognize the power that your imagination holds, and always has held, as the sole author of the fictions of your own life;*

This is the way to Truth.
This is the way to Love.
This is the way to God.

And all of these things are exactly what you are.

So, take as much time as you need to ride the waves of emotion that you are feeling right now. Pretend to be alone and disconnected from everything that makes you who you are for as long as you can stand it. And when you are ready for our next round of conversations, just let us know.

We are your curiosity.
We are your imagination.
We are your inner voice.

We are not dead, nor doth we sleep.
We are always within you and without you, surrounding you with love.

Until we meet again, dear friend. Adieu.

ABOUT THE AUTHOR

 GLENN OSTLUND is a writer and a podcaster who holds an M.A. in folklore and mythology from Indiana University. Glenn has hosted and produced the *Infants on Thrones* podcast since 2012. Glenn's other podcasts include: *Mytho-loGuy*, *The Enneagram Sandbox*, *The Spiritual Dimension of the Beatles*, and *Bathing with God*. Glenn is a proud father of three and lives with his partner outside of Phoenix, Arizona.

Made in the USA
Monee, IL
19 September 2020